J.A. Peehl

Land of Our Dreams

And other Verse

J.A. Peehl

Land of Our Dreams
And other Verse

ISBN/EAN: 9783337000240

Printed in Europe, USA, Canada, Australia, Japan

Cover: Foto ©Thomas Meinert / pixelio.de

More available books at **www.hansebooks.com**

THE UNDER SIDE OF THINGS

A Novel

BY

LILIAN BELL

AUTHOR OF "THE LOVE AFFAIRS OF AN OLD MAID"
"A LITTLE SISTER TO THE WILDERNESS" ETC.

NEW YORK
HARPER & BROTHERS PUBLISHERS
1896

> THE LOVE AFFAIRS OF AN OLD MAID. By
> LILIAN BELL. 16mo, Cloth, Ornamental, Uncut
> Edges and Gilt Top, $1 25.
>
> From its bright "Dedication" to its sweet and gracious close
> its spirit is wholesome, full of happy light, and one lingers over
> its pages.... Having read the book once, one will read it twice.
> —*Independent*, N. Y.
>
> PUBLISHED BY HARPER & BROTHERS, NEW YORK.

Copyright, 1896, by LILIAN BELL.

Copyright, 1896, by HARPER & BROTHERS.

All rights reserved.

THIS BOOK

Is Lovingly Dedicated to

MY SISTER

CLARA BELL LESSIG

WHO IS THE VERY PULSE OF MY HEART

CONTENTS

CHAPTER	PAGE
I. The Mother of Alice	1
II. A Small Town	13
III. Alice Goes to West Point	28
IV. Alice and Kate Vandevoort	38
V. Breakfast at Cozzens's	53
VI. Guard-Mounting	62
VII. Down Flirtation Walk	83
VIII. Counter-Irritants	103
IX. The Child Problem	121
X. On the Boat-House Steps	136
XI. The Battle of Stockbridge	160
XII. The Copeland Terrace	176
XIII. Alice's Wedding-Day	189
XIV. At Fort Hamilton	200
XV. The Fork in the Road	216
XVI. Into Silence	230

THE UNDER SIDE OF THINGS

I

THE MOTHER OF ALICE

It was written in the outlines of Mrs. Copeland's nose that she was a Code of Public Morals, which you would do well to investigate and live by. So remarkable was this eloquent feature that no description could bring it before you, no portrait do it full justice, because it shifted its position, not upon her face—pray do not misunderstand—but in its attitude towards the world. It needed not the cold grayness of her near-set eyes to accentuate its standard of Self, for if you could put your hand over her eyes, still you never would think of asking that nose for anything. No ill-clad, desperate man would beg her to visit his sick wife; no lost child ask her the way home. Had she been a man it would have been the nose of a money-getter, a money-lender, a usurer.

The peculiar thing about it was that it had no salient points by which to describe it. You could not recall her to a friend by referring to her nose, for it was neither hooked nor retroussé, but once you saw it you never forgot it. It meant so much of what had happened, and presaged so clearly what would happen. It was neither large nor thin nor high, and yet it was all three, but so cunningly were these attributes combined that you noticed without speaking of it. The nostrils were not thin to show sensitiveness. They were not thick. They were shapeless. And in a nose plainly intended by Nature to be pointed, there was an unexpected broadness in the end, which meant sufficiency unto itself, and a determined belief in the supremacy of her Ego over the Egoes of everybody else in the world. Her nose challenged your pedigree on the spot.

If you had your own life to live, and your own view of how to live it, Mrs. Copeland's nose became most annoying. There is a virtue so blatant that it becomes a vice. Hers was of that order. You felt that you ought to adopt it and that she thought so too, and that if you were in her family she would make you.

After one critical look at her nose you knew why George Copeland went to West Point when his father hoped he would be a lawyer. You knew why Alice Copeland, having been brought up by her mother, loved her father the best. You knew why the poor sometimes refused to accept blankets from her, which entitled her to order their whole future lives to suit herself. You knew why beggars occasionally threw her bread back in her face. You knew why she never gave generously, palms outward, but always with her hands turned in. You knew why, when she sent a sick friend a potted plant, she asked her to return the pot; or if she sent her jelly, she asked her to return the glass. You knew why she always walked to church on Sundays, rain or shine, with her black kid hands crossed over one another, her whole attitude that of an unrecognized martyr, her stiff skirts breathing the Pharisee's prayer. And if you were a weak-minded person, and Mrs. Copeland's way on a rainy Sunday lay by your house, you knew why you altered your feeble intention of staying at home, and why you went to church too.

Yet nobody ever discovered all this except Kate Vandevoort, who gave this description to Mollie Overshine after her first interview. But then Kate was frivolous. Everybody who did not know her said so.

This morning all that you could see of Judge Copeland across the breakfast-table was the Philadelphia *Press*. Undoubtedly he was behind it, for no paper, no matter how stiff its policy, could have sat up there alone. Besides, on either side of its outstretched pages you could see the judge's fingers, one of which wore an amethyst ring, with the crest of the Copelands embedded in it in tiny diamonds.

Mrs. Copeland sat opposite, behind the fat silver coffee urn, whose polished convex sides transformed her narrow, aristocratic countenance into an impertinent cartoon. It turned her long nose into the squat feature of a South African, and broadened her dignified mouth daringly. If that urn had not belonged to the Copelands for generations, Mrs. Copeland never would have tolerated the impudence of the caricature. As it was, she never permitted the butler to stand where he could obtain this view of her. She had been known to dismiss a maid without a moment's warning because upon first catching this glimpse of her new mistress in the coffee-urn she had burst out laughing, and, flinging her apron over her head, had rushed from the room in confusion. If Mrs. Copeland had possessed a sense of humor she might have forgiven the unfortunate creature. But the outrage to her sacred dignity was so great that it was only partially wiped out by ordering the poor maid's trunk set outside the gate in a pouring rain. She never knew that the judge quietly paid for the ruined clothes and a month's wages besides. And it was better so.

On one side of the table sat Alice Copeland. You would not consider her face unusual until you knew her. Then you wondered how she came to be so pretty. Her mother never realized how she absorbed Alice's personality. She still regarded her as a child.

Opposite to her, on the other side of the table, her younger brother squirmed. Gifford's years are of no importance. He was at the age when boys wriggle. George, the older boy, was at West Point, and breakfast was half over before little Elsie, long-legged, thin, and sallow, came in, with a martyred expression, and sat down without greeting any one. Mrs. Copeland permitted her to do this because she was shy. As a result, her manners were always atrocious.

"I see by the paper," said the judge, cheerfully, looking over the top of it, "that I have been appointed on the Board of Visitors to West Point."

The look of quiet pleasure faded from his face at his wife's distinct silence, and an anxious shade crossed it.

"That will be pleasant, I think, for then I can see George." He put forth this remark as one who was accustomed to apologize, not only for himself, but for existing circumstances.

Still no reply. Mrs. Copeland's knife grated harshly through her toast, then slipped and struck her plate. A faint flush suffused her face, the unmistakable flush of displeasure.

"Are you pleased, Mary?"

"I do not like to be informed of your movements through the columns of the newspapers," she said, icily.

"But that was only my way of telling you, dear. I thought it would be a little surprise."

"I do not like surprises."

"But I only did it for a jest."

"I do not like jests."

The judge's fine ruddy countenance paled a little. He stirred his coffee, eying it absently. "I would have told you if I myself had known it sooner," he said, looking up with a smile meant to propitiate her.

"This cannot be the first you have heard of it," she said, refusing his glance.

"No, but it is the first I knew of the appointment. I only knew that my name had been suggested."

"I think I might have been trusted with so important a piece of news."

The judge colored at her sarcastic emphasis.

"I know it is not much of an honor, dear, but you know I only accept these things on your account. I don't care for them myself. I would much rather attend to my flowers and stay quietly at home with you. You are my greatest attraction."

"That is right! Make me feel how much of your comfort you sacrifice for me," she said, ignoring the little compliment which many a woman would have hugged to her heart all day.

"Oh, my dear wife, I did not mean it that way. Pray pardon me. You surely could not think me so rude as to insinuate that anything I do for your pleasure is a sacrifice."

She compressed her thin lips without replying.

"Who makes these appointments, father?" asked Alice.

"The President appoints the visitors at large, and the Senate and House each appoints some of its members."

"It is very nice, I think, to be selected by the President, to have him reach down into private life in that way, and let you put a finger in the government pie. It makes you feel so American."

"And how else could one possibly feel when one is an American?" asked Mrs. Copeland, who was of Scotch descent.

"One can feel any nationality here in America, when everybody has more liberty than native-born Americans," said Alice.

Mrs. Copeland frowned, and Alice and her father exchanged sympathetic glances.

"I thought of taking you with me," he said to his daughter, with all a man's unwisdom as to when to broach a subject.

"Alice cannot go," said her mother.

The girl's face flashed and drooped in silence under these two sentences. She knew better than to urge or coax.

"I thought perhaps she might like it," said the judge, dubiously.

"It makes no difference whether she would like it if I think it unwise for her to go."

"But I thought it was time she began to see a little of the world," pursued the judge, anxious to vindicate his wisdom in the eyes of his wife. "She is eighteen. You were married at that age."

"I think it hardly chivalrous of you to remind me that I have a daughter as old as I was when I was married," said Mrs. Copeland, biting her words off with great distinctness. "You have an excellent way of reminding me that I am getting old. My mirror, however, anticipates the courtesy of my husband."

"Oh, my dear love, you misunderstood me. To me you are just as young and lovely as on our wedding-day, and Alice here is a surprise, a curious jest of Time. Alice, you must shorten your frocks.

It certainly is a mistake for me to have a grown daughter and a wife who looks even younger."

" You will see George in his uniform, Alice, if father takes you to West Point, and they have dress parade every afternoon, and all the cadets carry guns, and their mothers aren't there to ask 'em if they are loaded," put in Gifford, with a mutinous look at his mother. She smiled at this, for he was her idol, but she would not trust him even with the picture of a gun, much to his disgust.

" Alice is not going to West Point," she said. But it was a gentler tone, and every one's countenance brightened. Even the butler stepped more briskly. He was used to this sort of thing, however. He had been with the Copelands twelve years.

The judge, although scrupulously careful about his diet, had dyspepsia. Perhaps this was because he went through with a good deal at his meals besides eating, particularly at breakfast, which was a pity. Breakfast is bad enough in itself, without any one selecting that unfortunate time to be particularly disagreeable.

"Oh, let her go, mother! Let them both go, and we will stay at home together. Or, no—you take me to Philadelphia. You promised, because I had the measles. Now do!" cried the real diplomat of the family, scrambling from his chair and rushing up to her. He trod upon her dress, but she did not push him away.

"I'll see about it," she said.

"That means that you can go, Alice," he cried. "It always means that, when she says she will see about it."

Alice smiled without speaking.

"I'll go to Philadelphia, too," said little Elsie, suddenly.

Gifford's face clouded. Alice shook her head at him imperceptibly, and although he knew that Elsie's going would spoil everything for him, he smiled at her bravely.

"You are not well enough, Elsie," said Mrs. Copeland. "You look sallow. I think you ought not to have got up this morning."

Elsie stopped eating, and refused her third waffle. She was the sort of child whom you could make ill by telling her she looked so.

"I am ill, but I want to go," she whimpered.

Everybody looked up anxiously.

"Let her go, mother," said Gifford. "She'll have hysterics if you don't."

"Very well. You can go, Elsie. The poor child is able to take so few pleasures!" sighed Mrs. Copeland. Elsie's face, which had brightened at the prospect of Philadelphia, drew down to a proper degree of martyrdom at her mother's last words.

She had everything in the world she wanted, yet she was always referred to as "poor little Elsie Copeland." Alas, to waste the heavenly gift of pity upon the carefully suffering rich!

"I am afraid the noise and crowd of the city will frighten my little bird," said Mrs. Copeland, "and make her cry."

"No, it won't," said Elsie.

Perhaps it will not be anticipating too much to chronicle at this point that Elsie went with them, and began to cry in the train, so that by the time they were to begin the excursion which was Gifford's reward, Elsie was in strong hysterics, and had to be put to bed. Gifford spent the day with his little nose flattened against the hotel window, gazing into the street and winking back his tears. But he was growing used to it. Elsie always spoiled things for everybody wherever she went.

When Gifford and Alice were alone, after breakfast, Gifford seized her hand, saying in an undertone:

"I'll make her let you go to West Point, because you never told her that I went in swimming on Saturday. You said you were going to, but you didn't. That's just like a girl. And I'll make her let you and father both go."

"Perhaps you can't," said Alice, in a spiritless voice. "I couldn't."

"Ho! don't you know I can make her do anything? That is, anything except let *me* have any fun with guns and things. If I were father, I'd *make* her let me have a gun. He says I am old enough."

"*Make* her!" said Alice, aghast. "Nobody ever makes mother do anything. You oughtn't to speak so."

"Ho! you're only a girl," said Gifford, scornfully, which incontestable fact Alice did not attempt to disprove.

II

A SMALL TOWN

STOCKBRIDGE, Pennsylvania, is situated on the Delaware River. It was an old town even on the day when Alice Copeland was declared old enough to see a little of the world outside its narrow limits, and that was soon after the war, whose echoes were still reverberating in women's ears, and whose ragged wounds were still bleeding in women's hearts. In church the black-robed figures in mourning were silent witnesses of the grief and losses which Time had not yet wiped out. The quiet of the girl's life in conservative old Stockbridge had been rendered even more absolute for this reason, and her education had gone on without a break caused by anything more exciting than a game of croquet in the morning or a game of whist in the evening.

A small town in the East is as different from a small town in these later days in the West as black is from white. Their chief point of resemblance is that everybody knows everybody's else affairs. Otherwise let no one confuse the two.

In the West the broad open streets given by the generosity of the never-ending prairies, are symbolic of the town's radical hospitality. In the East the narrow, thrifty streets, jammed in between the hills and the sea, indicate the town's conservative selection of guests. In the West everything is new, nobody was born there, and the graveyards are fresh and small and bustling. In the East everybody was born there, everything is old, and the graveyards are large and stately and silent. In the West there is freshly turned sod and there are miles of barbed-wire fences. In the East there are stone walls and ivy and green mould and lichens.

In the West nobody knows who your grandfather was. In the East everybody knew your great grandfather. In the West to hustle is to be great. In the East everybody has time to be slow, and haste is inelegant. The provincialism of the West is uncouth and broad. The provincialism of the East is maddeningly narrow. The innate feeling of a young man from a small Western town that he is only one of a tremendous mass of humanity and that in order to be individualized he must boisterously assert himself, that because his family name is unknown in the great city he must shout it in your ear and begin each argument with the premise that he is just as good as anybody, springs from the nature of the new West. This newness largely consists of a broad, democratic brotherhood, which evidences itself in servants insisting upon being called "help" and upon dining with the family. In a town of the same size in the East, caste is recognized from the ancient order of things. The banker's son who goes to New York states his name modestly and expects it to be known. Very likely it is. If not, he is neither hurt nor offended. His place in the economy of the universe is secure even if a few do not know him. He goes on about his business quietly. It never would occur to him to insist that he was "as good as you are"—probably because, in his secret heart, very quietly and elegantly, he thinks himself much better! Both young fellows, being Americans, are at heart gentlemen. Their manners alone betray the difference in their environment, and neither is to blame. Both are creatures of circumstance and the natural product of their respective civilizations.

Because Alice Copeland had lived in the small town of Stockbridge all her life was no reason why she was provincial in the Western acceptation of the term. Her provincialism she inherited quite naturally from her mother, and it only took the mild form of a feeling of indifference to all the world except Stockbridge and Philadelphia. The names of the two towns may differ in various Eastern States, but their tolerance rarely gets beyond two, and when it does, it skips over to London and Paris. It never, for instance, comes to include three—their own, New York, and Boston, or their own, Philadelphia, and New York. For most Eastern people the trinity does not exist. They have fallen into a certain geographical unitarianism.

If Alice was narrow, it was a very gentle narrowness, neither obstinate nor froward. She was a Scotch Presbyterian because her mother was. Everybody knows that the Giffords of Philadelphia have always been Scotch Presbyterians. Alice never discussed the matter, but she believed in election and predestination, and honestly thought that no man could be saved unless he were equally firm in that faith, and safe within the fold of the Presbyterian church, with his name written upon the church-books in ink. Such simple, iron conviction admitted of no discussion.

Stockbridge had reason to be proud of one or two of its distinctions, which set it apart from its fellows. It boasted no theatre, but it had nine churches. Of course the Scotch Presbyterian was the most prosperous, because the Copelands belonged there.

Unsaved Baptists and Methodists, with their less handsome edifices, sometimes shook their heads over the luxuries of the Presbyterians, and smiled to think what old John Knox would have said to their cushions and velvet hangings and choir. But they never mentioned these things to Mrs. Copeland. Somehow Mrs. Copeland's nose did not invite impertinent home thrusts like these. But the truth of it was that this unusual spectacle of a rich church in those times was grounded in the same fundamental reasons which made the Copeland family unusual in other respects. Mrs. Copeland's Scotch blood made her give steadily to her church, and the judge's French blood caused him, if he gave at all, to give lavishly.

But there were counteracting influences which kept down the pride of the people in the godliness and chastity of their institutions, one of which was the constant illness of the inhabitants. These ailments seldom ended fatally. Indeed people died quite as often of old age or railroad accidents in Stockbridge as anywhere else, but surely no town could boast such varied chronic complaints, which just gently stirred people's sympathy to a healthy activity and gave them an excuse for visiting, as Stockbridge. Nearly everybody who was full-grown, and there were also quite a goodly number of non-dangerous infantile disorders, had his own private malady, which was as distinctive and peculiarly his own, and as unavailable to others, as his silver door-plate. Indeed, for one family to lap over into another family's complaint without adding a complication which made it individual would have been regarded as impertinent a trespass upon sacred privacy as for a man to copy his neighbor's grave decoration in the church-yard.

On the evening of the day when Alice's visit to West Point was trembling in the balance a small excitement took place in the visit of Colonel and Mrs. Christopher Overshine.

The Overshines were next in importance to the Copelands, but just now the Overshines were in a position to cast a lustre by their presence upon even the Copelands. Mrs. Overshine, knowing the importance of having a piece of news like a divorce almost in their immediate family, for John Vandevoort was her own second cousin, had held aloof from everybody, even from Mrs. Copeland, to whom her friends always told everything first, as became her station, for something like ten days, much to Mrs. Copeland's secret annoyance. Outside gossip was scarce, of course, in a town like Stockbridge, where nothing ever happened. Still Mrs. Copeland thought there was no sense in Mrs. Overshine's acting as if she were the ark of the covenant just because she was in the inner circle of a celebrated

New York divorce case. And when on Sunday Mrs. Overshine went so far as to keep her veil down all during the sermon, as if being related to the Vandevoorts made her sacred, and afterwards made her way out of church to her carriage with her head down, speaking to nobody, Mrs. Copeland's grenadier spirit actually chafed under the restraint which Christianity imposed.

Now, however, the Overshines were coming up the walk. Mrs. Copeland, knowing, of course, that this was Mrs. Overshine's first visit since the details of the divorce came, forgave her impertinence of Sunday, and even felt a sort of respect for the *coup d'état* which had made the presence of Mrs. Overshine of more importance than that of any other woman in Stockbridge.

It was a pleasure to see Judge Copeland greet his guests. After you had taken the colorless fingers of Mrs. Copeland, it was like floating out into the Gulf Stream to look into his keen blue eyes and to see him bend over your hand and to hear his courtly, " Good-day, madam."

The Copeland house was colonial, and set well back on a handsome terrace fronting the river. From all the windows you could look down upon the sinuous and tricky Delaware winding its indolent way to the sea. Indeed, as if to accommodate so influential a family as the Copelands, it even made a gracious bend, and wandered past the dining-room windows, so that from all over the house you had the loveliest view of its friendly ways.

Colonel Overshine limped to the window.

"The old Delaware is quite high just now, Judge. It doesn't look as though it would ever get so low that the dust would blow off it."

"No, no; it does not. It looks to me as though it were deep enough to float the *Kennebunk*. It is a great pity our river is not navigable up here."

"You are right. It would straighten out a good deal of that snarl about freight rates if the river would step in and say, 'Here, use me.'"

"It would so. How is your knee, Colonel? This damp weather give you an extra twinge now and then?"

"Oh yes. But I am getting used to it. You can get used to anything, you know, Judge. A man could get used to hanging if he were hanged every day."

"Bad place to have a ball, Colonel. Never fails to leave a stiff knee. John Feversham—you know Feversham who was colonel of the Thirteenth Rhode Island and is now captain in the regular army?—he had a stiff knee for two years, but he got rid of it in some way. He's all right now."

"Gad, I wish I knew how he did it," said Colonel Overshine, sitting down, his lame leg stretched out stiffly before him. "I hear about these marvellous cures, but I never see them. Every once in a while me wife discovers a sure cure for a bald head. But look at mine. Me two complaints are a bald head and a lame leg, and I expect to die in full possession of both of them."

The maid entered with a tray. Mrs. Copeland, being a total abstainer, never served wine to her guests, but there was sure to be lemonade and cocoanut cake in abundance.

"And she began to behave badly soon after they were married," Mrs. Overshine was saying.

Both men forgot what they were talking about and listened.

"Me wife's cousin, John Vandevoort," murmured Colonel Overshine.

"I have no patience with John that he did not take her in hand at once," said Mrs. Copeland, who loved to direct other people's families.

"Yes; but you know John. He is too gentle and lovely to take a fly in hand, let alone that woman, who, as you know, is a wonderfully attractive creature when she wants to be; accomplished, clever, sings well, and they say she has written a book."

Mrs. Copeland threw up both hands. "Poor John!" she said. "Is it published?"

"No; and it may never be, now."

Mrs. Copeland gave a sigh of relief. Things

were very bad indeed with poor John Vandevoort, but not as bad as they might be.

"She is perfectly well and strong, I believe," said Mrs. Copeland, "so John has not had illness to contend with."

"Oh no; she has some trouble which causes her to go into hysterics every time she loses her temper. She gets violent at times. John says he thinks her mind is affected."

"Mind!" said Mrs. Copeland. "Temper! I know her. I saw her when I went to New York to hear Sontag. She weighed nearly two hundred pounds last winter, if I am any judge of weight from seeing a woman in so shameless an evening dress as she wore."

"I think so too. If John only had made a stand when they were first married! He says he couldn't. When he told me of some of her tantrums I said to him, 'John, a good shaking would do her good.' And he said, 'Cousin Mollie, she is the mother of my children.' Now you know I couldn't say a word after that."

"Children? I thought there was only one."

"No, two; Frances and Margaret—Peggy, they call her."

"What will be done with them?"

"John says I am to have them for a time."

"And bring them here?"

" Yes."

Mrs. Copeland cleared her throat in a pleased way. She was glad she was going to *see* some of this trying and sad affair.

" Where is Alice?" asked Mrs. Overshine.

Mrs. Copeland eyed her sharply, knowing that Mrs. Overshine knew and was overjoyed at the knowledge that Alice was out with Frank Overshine. Mrs. Overshine only wanted to make Mrs. Copeland admit it.

" She went to the archery meeting, I believe."

" No, the Archery Club meets on Friday. This is only Tuesday."

" Oh, then it must have been the Canoe Club."

" Did she go alone?"

" No, Ellen St. Francis went with her."

" And did those two girls go alone?"

" No, one of the young boys in the neighborhood went with them."

Mrs. Overshine retired from the field, and rocked her chair in exasperated silence.

" That is a handsome ring you have on, Judge," said Colonel Overshine. " Have I ever seen it before?"

" I think not. My wife gave it to me on my last birthday," said the judge, taking it off and handing it to him.

" Very fine stone. What is the design?"

Judge Copeland leaned back in his chair, set his finger tips together, and looked at the ceiling. Mrs. Copeland laid down her fancy work. She was never without either her fancy work or her Bible. If laid out in a straight line, she must have done miles of fancy work. If read in a straight line, she must have read miles in her Bible.

She rested her long slim hands, glittering with rings, upon her crewel-work—which in after-years passed through the various stages of fashionable fancy work, through silk knitting, tatting, card-board embroidery, and from that into centrepieces and drawn-work—and Colonel Overshine looked towards her. Mrs. Overshine went on rocking rather aggressively. She knew exactly what Mrs. Copeland was about to tell. She had heard it before, dozens of times. She knew just how she would tell it, how deprecating she would look at the mention of the count's name, as who should say, " Of course we are not to blame for having a count among our ancestors," and she knew how she would pause and lower her voice before mentioning the duke's name, for here the narrative grew really sacred. She knew it all, and followed it word by word as Mrs. Copeland began.

"That ring, Colonel, contains the crest of the Copeland family. Copeland is French, you know, and was originally Copelin. The descent of the judge's branch of the family is very direct through the Comte de Copelin, clear back to the Duc de Copelin, his most famous ancestor."

Mrs. Copeland never went further back than the Duc de Copelin, for if she had done so she must inevitably have soiled her clean Presbyterian lips by the admission that the famous duke's mother had been a court favorite under Louis XIV., who had created her Duchesse de Copelin, and laid the foundation of the Copeland fortune by the presentation of the estates, which had since, however, passed into other hands and bear another name.

She could not be expected to admit that the Copeland family crest, embroidered by her own fingers upon every piece of linen in the house, from sheets and table-cloths down to doilies and handkerchiefs, had had its origin in such a blot upon the family honor.

"Very fine," said Colonel Overshine.

"We have records," proceeded Mrs. Copeland, with dignity, "of the military exploits of these famous men, especially those of the Duc de Copelin."

"Me wife has all the ancestors in our family," said Colonel Overshine, with ill-placed jocularity; "all I know of mine is that me grandfather was hanged for being a pirate."

It is an old joke, but one very dear to the heart

of the American man whose wife is interested in family trees.

Mrs. Copeland colored with displeasure. Mrs. Overshine smiled. The colonel's grandfather had been governor of Rhode Island. Judge Copeland, although relieved to have the oft-repeated narrative broken off, looked anxiously at his wife, but she had taken up her fancy work again, and had retired from the conversation. She turned her attention back to Mrs. Overshine.

"What will become of Emily after she gets her divorce?"

"I am sure I don't know."

"How distressing that she left him and now sues on the ground of desertion."

"Very."

"Will he contest it?"

"I think not."

"He could, though," put in Colonel Overshine. "He has plenty of grounds against her, but he will not. He says he did not marry her to take advantage of a woman's weakness. It is exasperating to hear him talk. All he wants is to have the custody of the children. She is capricious and utterly irresponsible. One week she loves them to death, and the next week they never see her. They are the sweetest, cleverest, worst children I ever saw; keen as razors, honest as the day—just like John—own up to anything they have done, and the older one, Frances, is as pretty as a picture."

Just then Gifford Copeland burst into the room.

"Softly, my son," said the judge.

"Good-evening, Mrs. Overshine. There are two children and a lady at your house. They have just come in on the train. And they want to see you immediately!"

Mrs. Overshine rose hastily.

"I wonder if it can be Emily?" said Mrs. Copeland.

"It would be just like her to come into our house with her family, and fight our cousin, her husband, from under our roof," growled Colonel Overshine.

"Let me know if it is Emily," said Mrs. Copeland, at the door.

"Very well. Perhaps I'll send you word by 'one of the young boys in the neighborhood,'" said Mrs. Overshine, sweetly.

Mrs. Copeland smiled. She always smiled when another woman showed temper.

III

ALICE GOES TO WEST POINT

IN some way, Gifford had managed it as he said he would, and Alice was going to West Point.

Gifford and his sister were on more friendly terms than many small boys and their older sisters. There was an open-hearted, chivalrous generosity about Gifford which would make his way through life quite easy, and there was a gentleness about Alice which appealed to the native manliness in Gifford, and made him want to "look out for Alice." He considered her just the kind of a girl to be imposed upon, and, young as he was, he already had begun to stand between her and her mother, who was the one who profited most acutely by Alice's sweetness.

Gifford came out to the carriage-step to see them off. Mrs. Copeland was up-stairs with a headache, a dark room, and smelling-salts.

It was so early in the morning the horses tossed their heads impatiently and stamped their slim hoofs, for it was a glorious day.

"Are you all right, sis?" asked Gifford, helping her in.

"Yes, thank you, dear. Don't be disappointed that mother is too ill to take you to Philadelphia."

"Ho, we'll go before you get back. Don't you worry about that. Good-bye, good-bye. Have a good time, and don't you come home until you want to, Alice. I'll take care of mother for you. Good-bye!"

He kept shouting after the carriage until it was lost to view around a bend.

The river road to the station is so beautiful that it hurts you. It makes your throat ache and your eyes smart, and you have to swallow hard and often, for the beauty of it goes to your heart.

The Delaware was at her best, high and proud, yet full of a tender humility under the caresses of the morning, like a proud woman conscious of her own beauty, yet willing to bend her pride to gentleness under the influence of love.

Father and daughter drove nearly all the way in silence, conscious of each other's fulness of heart, and unwilling to break the spell by trivialities. Sometimes they looked at each other and smiled, and once, when they made a sudden turn which flashed into view a long, narrow island almost covered with green grass, like a great emerald marquise ring set in the centre of the river, Alice slipped her little gloved hand into her father's with sympathetic understanding.

Pacing up and down the station platform, waiting for the same train they were to take, Alice saw a tall young woman, whose black veil, dropping from her little round hat, concealed her features, and only revealed at the back a wealth of auburn hair, dressed in the prevailing fashion, resembling a peck measure. Her waist was the smallest, her crinoline the largest, her skirts the most voluminous that Alice ever had seen. Her whole costume had "New York" stamped as unmistakably upon it as were the modest folds of Alice Copeland's labelled " Stockbridge, Pennsylvania." She was tall and sweeping, and Alice thought she never had seen anything so graceful as the way she walked and managed her skirts. Alice watched her all the way to New York, for without being nervous or vivacious, she was always moving—always doing something worth looking at. Everybody else was looking at her too, for although her veil was still down, she had the assured manners of a beauty, and she seemed to exercise a certain fascination upon every one in the car who sat within range of her.

Her own carriage was waiting for her, and she gave no directions, only nodded to the footman in answer to his salute, stepped in ; the door slammed,

the man sprang upon the box, folded his arms—
and they were off.

Alice actually sighed as she disappeared. She
was foolish and young and still had her ideals. Oh,
lovely age, no matter when it comes, when we can
watch a fellow-traveller under a veil and fancy her
beautiful enough to love and believe her good
enough to follow to the ends of the earth!

Keep it, Alice Copeland, as long as you can. It
means much more than an idle infatuation. It
means youth, and innocence, and unshattered ideals,
and the song of birds and eternal spring-time in
one's life. Be foolish and unwise while you can.
Once you lose the capacity, it never comes again.
Once you begin to know, you begin to hate. What
need have butterflies and lambs and song-birds
and young girls of wisdom?

"Venus went to Minerva, and said, 'Teach me
wisdom.' 'If I do,' said Minerva, 'you never again
can be the Goddess of Love.'"

Judge Copeland always went to the Astor House
when in New York. He had been going to the Astor
House for twenty-five years. He had seen it in its
jubilee days, before the war, when all the Southern
society girls spent their winters there, when it occupied a proud position in the way of celebrated
beauties and aristocratic inmates. It was the ral-
lying place for all the flower and wealth of the

South, and it witnessed such scenes of gayety among first families as now only occur in country-houses during the season. No hotel has ever been in this respect what the Astor House was before the war. It was like a great house party, with all the privacy of one's own apartments, or all the friendliness one chose to bestow.

Although much of its glory had departed, Alice enjoyed any large hotel too much to be a captious critic, nor was she one to seek after strange gods. The old, the established order of things suited her simple tastes better than the fashionable and newer hotels to which most girls would have inclined.

After dinner they went to see Charlotte Cushman as Meg Merrilies.

Alice never forgot that night. She sat in a box for the first time in her life, and lost herself so completely in the play, and the dazzling rows of lights, and the music, and the sense of being removed from the people and of being in some way different from all that she ever had been before, that she paid little heed to the gentleman in their box—a certain Senator Cobb, from Ohio, one of their party on the Board of Visitors. After one glance Alice hardly looked at him. She was no judge of art; for in that one glance she decided that he might be a youngish man who looked old, or an oldish man who looked young.

But Senator Cobb, so far from feeling hurt by her indifference, was piqued into more acute interest in her than perhaps otherwise he might have felt. The few years which had elapsed since his accession to the Senate and his wife's death had been filled so full of attentions from ladies possessing three eyes—their own and a weather eye, for the senator's fortune was so large it was nebulous —that it seemed to him he always had been an eligible and the recipient of this manifest interest. It is so easy for one's Ego to grow accustomed to spelling itself with a capital, and to forget that one's old friends had hitherto always spelled it with a small letter.

The truth of it was that the Cobbs, of Phœnix, Ohio, were plain and simple folk. The first year in Washington had killed the faithful little woman who had stood shoulder to shoulder with her husband through all their unfortunate years, slaving at work much too hard for her, and keeping up his spirit until coal was discovered right under the very mortgage, you might say, which they were trying to lift. It proved to have such power of raising things that it blew not only the mortgage from overhead, but it lifted the Cobbs into social and political power in Phœnix with such force that it finally landed them in Washington.

Perhaps it is hardly fair, for the honor of our national politics, to ascribe all this to coal—for the senator possessed undoubted ability, and made a very good senator as senators go. But it *is* safe to say that except for the coal Joel Cobb's abilities would never have been discovered by the enthusiastic citizens of Phœnix. And yet, when all is said, it does not require either coal or enthusiasm or ability to make of a candidate "a dark horse." And it was as the "dark horse" that Joel Cobb found himself in the Senate.

Once in Washington, however, the coal was of inestimable benefit—except that the social swim into which it floated them sucked down his poor little adoring wife and left him a widower.

But he was not an unusual man on certain lines, consequently he never knew that anything except Washington life had killed her. Neither did he know that she had worked too hard. Neither did he know that it was her indomitable pluck and encouragement that had kept a roof over their heads until coal could be discovered. It was as if her grip on affairs had only lasted until some one else would take the helm. For when she began to rest it was the beginning of the long rest. Her resting-time came too late.

The senator did not know this, nor would he believe it if he could read this veracious history, for it would be a difficult as well as an unkind thing to dislodge the idea of his own importance, seeing that he derived his chief happiness in life from fostering that harmless fallacy. It would have upset his dignity and hurt his vanity to give any credit for his career to the exhausted little woman who slept in the graveyard at Phœnix beside her crippled boy. Indeed, his most famous campaign speech contained these stirring lines:

"Single-handed and alone, from a poor, unknown boy following the plough day after day, season after season, with no encouragement from man, woman, or child, with not one hand held out to offer the help I so sorely needed, poor, ignored, uncared for, I, a simple farmer's lad, with only my country's good at heart, dreamed great dreams of this hour, and hewed my unaided way to success. (Loud applause.)

"Single-handed and alone have I risen step by step, with only brain and brawn to aid me. But, buoyed up by the noble motto 'Pro bono publico,' I come before you at this time to lay whatever wealth I may have built up, my highest powers of heart and head, at my country's feet, and to serve her to the best of my ability in any capacity to which she may see fit to call me." (Prolonged applause.)

It was a great speech, although, of course, this is only a sample, and, perhaps, an unfair one. It was much more impressive and stirring to hear him deliver it; for there he stood before them, a living example to all other poor boys who, like him, single-handed and alone have hewed or are hewing their way to fame and fortune with no assistance from their toiling, moiling wives, if they happen to have such a bit of machinery in the house.

Senator Cobb, however, possessed many of the qualifications of the successful politician, one of which he displayed in the tact he employed with Alice Copeland on that night when he first met her. For, during the play, seeing that she was absorbed, he contented himself with looking at her. But at the little supper afterwards, whither they betook themselves, he made himself exceedingly agreeable for an old gentleman—Alice had a better light on him then—and she was grateful to him for taking such an interest in her and her simple affairs.

Had Alice been less modest or more self-conscious, she might have seen that several, other than Senator Cobb, fixed their eyes on the fresh-complexioned girl in the front of the box who sat so still and followed the play with such breathless interest, among them the same tall young woman with auburn hair who had travelled with her from Stockbridge. She watched Alice through her opera-glasses, and seemed bored by her companions, but Alice was too far off and too much absorbed to recognize her.

The next morning, just as they were leaving for the boat, a great box from the florist's was sent to Alice with Senator Cobb's card in it. She gave a little cry of delight when she opened it. Instead of roses, it was filled with spring flowers—crocuses, jonquils, hyacinths, lilies-of-the-valley, heliotrope, and mignonette. The very breath of spring came with it, and rose and floated out through the room.

"What a nice old gentleman!" she said to her father, who was bending over the flowers scarcely less enchanted than she. "But what shall I do with them?"

"Oh, we must take them with us. See how they seem to watch us out of their little faces. Flowers are almost human, Alice, especially these baby spring flowers. Of course we must take them."

So their way to the boat was traced by a very small black man bearing a very large white box, which was deposited with more care and far more minute instructions than they bestowed upon their luggage. Then they went on deck and leaned over the railing, watching the boat put off from her pier, and steam her slow way between all the other craft, in the first stage of her beautiful journey up the Hudson.

IV

ALICE AND KATE VANDEVOORT

ELDERLY admirers with unctuous manners and an oily skin can make themselves very revolting to sensitive young ladies with romantic tendencies. It was on this journey that the mentally dwarfing fact was forced even upon Alice Copeland's unsuspicious nature that Senator Cobb—her "nice old gentleman"—had sent her those flowers in the guise of a suitor. This startling discovery so upset Alice's usually gentle equilibrium that the lovely journey was completely spoiled for her—in point of fact, she hardly saw it.

No one knows what the senator said to her. The only evidences of her discomfort to be seen were the scarlet cheeks and downcast eyes of the girl while Senator Cobb was talking to her. He must have given her quite plainly to understand his intentions concerning her, as elderly admirers with large fortunes have a little way of doing, for the moment she could escape from him she hurried to his box of flowers, and, watching for a favorable moment, she nerved herself to the ordeal of throwing the whole thing overboard in the wake of the steamer.

Alice thought no one had seen her, for it was near dusk, but a tall young woman with auburn hair was sitting in the shadow and watching her with amused eyes. Evidently she was clever at understanding situations, for she clapped her gloved hands softly together, and whispered " Good " under her breath, and half rose as if to go to the girl, then sank back in her place, shaking her head as if at her own folly.

Alice Copeland was an odd girl. She could nerve herself to a display of spirit like the flinging of that box of flowers away, but she could not bring herself to tell her father why. When he discovered their loss and asked after them in much the same tone of anxiety he would have used if Gifford had disappeared, Alice admitted that she had thrown them overboard.

"Thrown them overboard? Why, Alice, child, what is the matter with you? Are you ill? To throw flowers overboard! Why didn't you give them to some one? Why didn't you tell me? I would have removed them."

"They smelled too sweet," said Alice, with a show of petulance quite foreign to her.

She looked suspiciously at her father to see if he knew of any cause, but he, being a man, had seen nothing. He regarded her anxiously, however, and felt her hands to see if she were feverish.

Their arrival at West Point was likewise marred for Alice in that George did not prove the haven of refuge that she had hoped, but both he and his father seemed pleased to allow Senator Cobb to look after her wraps and to constitute himself her escort. This willing acquiescence on their part so wrought upon Alice, together with the fatuous attentions of the senator, that she lost what little self-control she ordinarily possessed, and allowed her anxiety to be seen plainly in her face.

That evening, when the commandant and many of the cadets flocked to Cozzens's to call upon the visitors, Alice was handed about from one to another of her father's friends, meeting them mechanically, bowing to them like an automaton, and all the time wishing herself well back in Stockbridge. She felt that she could even endure the obnoxious attentions of Frank Overshine, who *would* wear hats so large for him that they touched his ears. She thought indulgently of his wide mouth—the kind of a mouth which always goes with a frank, open countenance and that sort of a hat—when she compared his capabilities of being snubbed into faint-heartedness with the confident smile of Senator Cobb and his deadly habit of "washing his hands in invisible soap," which so held Alice's eyes that she could not leave off looking at them.

She had been cornered by the senator all that first evening. She had seen the gray-coated cadets pass to and fro. She had met a number of her brother's friends. She had answered fully fifty times the question as to what kind of a journey she had, with a mechanical "Very pleasant, thank you," and had said "yes" to another fifty who wanted to know if this was her first visit to West Point. She remembered none of their names. The cadets all looked alike to her. It seemed to her as though there were hundreds of white duck trousers and gray coats with brass buttons. She said over and over that she had seen nothing of West Point, but she thought she should like it very much. And the young fellows who asked her these intelligent questions were somewhat puzzled by her pleading blue eyes, and it almost stirred one or two of them to promise to do anything for her if she would only speak out and tell them what she wanted. And all the time her father and George were near by and saw nothing of her distress, and all the time Senator Cobb stood guard at her elbow and allowed no one to displace him, until suddenly into the room walked a tall young woman in a white dress with yellow roses at her belt and one against her bronze hair. She seemed to know everybody, bowing and smiling with perfect ease and unconcern to those who thronged around her, but moving slowly yet surely to where Alice Copeland sat with her wistful eyes drinking in the beauty of the newcomer, who finally paused just in front of her, looking down and smiling in such a frank and friendly way that Alice flushed and rose to her feet and smiled back at her quite as if she had known her always.

Senator Cobb rose also, and stood with his hands under his coat-tails and a nervous smile on his face.

"The senator will not introduce us, you see, Miss Copeland, because he knows that I have come to usurp his place and to talk to you myself; but on the whole, he shall be punished for monopolizing you, and shall be obliged to be the means of his own discomfiture, as my old black mammy used to make her little children go and cut the switches they presently were to be whipped with. Pray present us, Mr. Senator."

She paused and looked down at Senator Cobb from her greater height, and smiled brilliantly while waiting with her head rather haughtily poised.

The senator recognized her attitude and flushed as he said: "Delighted, I'm sure. Miss Copeland, allow me to present Miss Vandevoort."

Miss Vandevoort took both of Alice's hands in hers, and sat down beside her in the senator's chair.

"Thank you, dear Senator Cobb," she said, sweetly. "Now will you go and talk to Mrs. Verry and let me tell Miss Copeland who I am?"

She looked after his retreating figure, and laughed mischievously as she saw Alice's bewildered face.

"My dear," she said, leaning towards her with an engaging air, "you should be a little older to understand just how deliciously malicious we two have been to each other."

"Malicious?" said Alice. "How?"

"Should you really care to know? Wouldn't it be better for you to go on having life present itself pictorially, or do you care for the seamy side of the canvas?"

Miss Vandevoort was watching her narrowly. She knew just how much of a risk was involved in trying the intelligence of a Madonna-faced girl like Alice Copeland. Too often she had drawn a blank.

But a flash of comprehension swept over Alice's countenance as she said, "I want the seamy side."

"It is not beautiful, nor so innocent as the picture side."

"But it is more interesting. It is better to know it," answered Alice.

"More interesting, certainly; and better to know it at my age; hardly at yours."

"But let me begin with this, anyway. Tell me just how there was anything malicious in what I saw," urged Alice, not quite understanding how she dared to talk so freely, yet confident that her freedom was welcome to Miss Vandevoort.

"You could not see below the surface?"

"Not at all. I am very stupid, I suppose."

"No, not stupid; for this was very subtle and very trivial—not worth a sentence of this talk; but I'll tell you if you care to know. In the first place Senator Cobb had monopolized you to an extent not permissible in polite society, and, in spite of coming from a small town in Ohio, he was conscious that he had brazened out the well-bred efforts of three or four people who saw your flag of distress and tried to dislodge him. Then when I came and insisted, as only a woman can, and he saw defeat staring him in the face, he introduced me to you, instead of you to me—which, as I said before, is a mere bagatelle—but I spiked his guns again by saying that if he would leave us I would tell you who I was. Then to add insult to injury, I sent him to Mrs. Verry, who paid him such marked attention all last winter that people in Washington were driven to wondering if her intentions were honorable."

"Driven to wondering what?"

"Oh, driven to wondering if anything would come

of it. You see she is quite *prononcée*, and the affections of such a woman as that are not to be trifled with with impunity."

Alice relaxed and laughed. There was something very alluring about Miss Vandevoort's daring words, contrasted with her voice and manner. She seemed to be amused at everything. She reviewed everybody in the room for Alice's benefit, telling her who and what they were. Suddenly she turned to the girl, whose reserve seemed completely to have vanished under her raillery, and said, " Frank Overshine would have bored me to death talking of you if what he said had not interested me."

"Frank Overshine?" said Alice, coloring and drawing off.

"Yes. You see I know more about you than you do about me. I have been in Stockbridge for three days. I went down on a queer errand. I captured my brother John's children and took them down to Cousin Mollie Overshine's. You know Emily is getting a divorce from John, for which Heaven be praised. She had the children. John wanted them. Couldn't get them. Lawyers couldn't get them. Court couldn't get them. Emily is sharper than a dozen of John's lawyers. I said nothing, but I watched my chance, and when Emily went out one day I picked up the little tots and whisked them down to Stockbridge before anybody could wink. There was nobody else to do it, so I did it. I always have to do things that nobody else will do. The children were delighted to go with me. I could have taken them to Africa—they would have gone. I had to send to your house to get Cousin Mollie the evening I arrived, do you remember?"

"I remember the evening Mrs. Overshine was at our house and was sent for, but I was not there."

"True. I remember now Frank told me that he had you that evening."

"But another girl was with us," said Alice, eagerly, trying to disclaim young Overshine's ownership.

"So Frank said," answered Miss Vandevoort in a tone so droll that Alice was obliged to smile rather against her will. She disliked to make a jest of anything so serious as a love affair. She was very young.

"Poor Frank," sighed Miss Vandevoort in mock sympathy. "He is in a very bad way. His symptoms are quite aggravated. But it is a first attack."

Alice was silent with embarrassment and displeasure. She wondered how so radiant a creature as Miss Vandevoort could—could talk in this flippant way. It seemed to her Stockbridge sensibility almost indelicate.

"He is so hopeless about you too. How can you

bring yourself to flirt with him if you mean to take him in the end?"

"Take him?" cried Alice, hotly. "I never thought of such a thing!"

"Ah, that was what I wanted to know," answered Miss Vandevoort, calmly. "I wondered if it were a preferred suitor which made you treat poor Senator Cobb so cavalierly."

Alice was almost ready to cry with vexation. She felt as powerless to help herself with Miss Vandevoort as she had with the senator.

"You are flying another signal of distress," said Miss Vandevoort. "If the senator sees it he will come and dislodge me."

Alice's hands flew to her scarlet cheeks in sudden fear, and she stole a look around the room as if to locate the senator and the nearest door.

"Look here, my dear," said Miss Vandevoort, sitting up very straight and closing her fan. "Don't look so wretched. Don't allow situations to overpower you so. You are here, and unless you rise to the occasion you are going to miss all the pleasure your father has tried to give you, and you are going to allow these other girls to wrest the victory from you which you may have if you will. Now I have only been jesting with you, to try your mettle and to get my own bearings. Pull yourself together and get command of the situation, and I will give you the best time you ever had in your life. You will have so many beaux that you won't be able to manage them."

"I don't want them," said Alice, quickly. "I shouldn't know what to do with them. It would make me most unhappy."

"Is it so?" said Miss Vandevoort, slowly. "Well, I never thought of that possibility. I wonder what would have become of me if I had been brought up in Stockbridge."

"I do not like young men," said Alice. "They are so—so foolish. I would much rather talk to you occasionally, and let the other girls triumph over me if they want such a small victory as that would be."

Miss Vandevoort sat looking at her fan, and only nodded her head slowly in reply. Alice went on.

"Let Mrs. Verry have Senator Cobb, and let the other girls have the cadets—they all look bewilderingly alike to me—and whenever you want me to enjoy myself you come and talk to me. It is a good deal to ask, but you are so kind as to say that you want me to have a good time, and that is what I should like best."

Miss Vandevoort looked at Alice Copeland with interest. Yes, without doubt, she was the prettiest girl in the room, and she had about her a little well-bred air, which just missed being Quakerish by the spirited lift of her head, and just missed being vivacious by the subduing effects of Presbyterianism and Stockbridge, Pennsylvania. People often said of this quite satisfactory combination, "What a little lady Alice Copeland is."

"But you must dance to-morrow night at the hop," said Miss Vandevoort.

"What hop?"

"What hop? Oh, shades of my Puritan ancestors! What a bit of rural verdure it is! Why, the graduates' hop—the hop of the year—the hop all these Baltimore and Washington and New York girls have come up for—and the hop they all think you came for."

"Well, if I go I suppose that George will dance with me once or twice, and my father will take me in to supper, so that is all that is necessary—it is all I care for," said Alice.

"But your first hop at West Point? Why, child, some girls would give their two eyes and their two ears to be in your shoes."

"Would they? And do you care so much for such things? Why do you come?"

"I? Oh, I—I come because—I come because—because I like the army. I like to see the young fellows," said Miss Vandevoort, coloring and moving her head restlessly.

"Then you must know nearly everybody here," said Alice.

"I do. I know them all, I think."

"Well, are they all as much alike as they look?"

Alice's confidential tone amused Miss Vandevoort, and she laughed.

"No, indeed. Some are quite different. Some are really charming. There is one whom I am especially fond of."

Miss Vandevoort's frankness did not shock Alice this time. She looked more like a goddess to the girl than a woman, anyway. Alice only wondered who the fortunate young fellow could be, whom Miss Vandevoort would distinguish by so great a compliment as to declare herself fond of him. It was not that she seemed so much older either, which made her speech sound perfectly proper. It was more that she seemed a degree removed from all the rest, and in some way privileged. She had the confidence, in her daring, of an acknowledged belle, which in itself is a charm unless allowed to be stupidly prominent. Miss Vandevoort seemed to have the natural art of only delicately suggesting this, by the nice way in which she appeared to impart it to each one as an appeal to the subtlety of his intelligence, which invited him to catch this clue that she threw out and to make the most of it.

"Is he here to-night?" asked Alice, with more curiosity than she yet had shown about anybody.

Just then Miss Vandevoort looked up and bowed to him.

"No," she said, frankly doctoring the truth for the sake of the future. She held Alice's eyes with hers while she made an imperceptible movement of her fan, which the young man promptly obeyed. As he made his way slowly towards them Miss Vandevoort said to Alice:

"Now I wonder if you will prove equal to this situation. Senator Cobb is becoming restless under the caressing glances of the brilliant Verry, and he contemplates returning to the charge here. I have defended you all I can, but I will introduce one of the dearest fellows on earth to you, and if you are not clever enough to hold him here, Senator Cobb will get you again, and if you let him, I wash my hands of you. The best way to recommend this young man to so *difficile* a person as yourself is to guarantee that he is different. He graduates third from the head of his class and he is first captain of the corps of cadets. No such colossal glory as the latter will ever come to him in after years should he even become President. Ah, here you are! Captain Counselman, allow me to present you to Miss Copeland, the daughter of that most charming man, Judge Copeland, and the sister of your classmate. Probably you will not be allowed to remain unmolested long, as I have had daggers driven into me by the black eyes of Mr. Drake for the last ten minutes. He is even now glaring at me from the doorway, so hold the fort while you may, for there is no telling when you may be routed by the enemy."

When Alice ventured to raise her eyes above the brass buttons on his coat, he was half smiling at Miss Vandevoort and half frowning at Drake. Then he turned and looked down at her.

She afterwards wondered if it were that he really did stand straighter than all the others, or that he was taller, or that there was that look from his gray eyes under their level brows, or what it was that made her forget George, and her father, and Senator Cobb and Drake, and even Miss Vandevoort, and only remember that a face had come into her life which would remain with her, sleeping or waking, wherever she went, crowding everything in the world into a background for just this one face—the face of "the dearest fellow on earth," and one who was "different."

V

BREAKFAST AT COZZENS'S

MUCH to Alice's bewilderment the next morning, as she and her father walked into breakfast, she saw people bowing to her whom she had no recollection of meeting and whose names were a sealed book. Their table was the one farthest from the door, and to reach it they had to run the gantlet of the whole dining-room.

Mrs. Verry, in a brilliant scarlet dress, had the first table, which commanded a fine view of the door, and gave her an excellent opportunity to waylay any whom she chose to entice. Beside her plate lay a small bunch of red carnations. Everything about her was so intense that it almost made you wink.

"Who was that impossible person who bowed to us, daughter?" asked her father.

"A Mrs. Verry," answered Alice.

"An excellent name; quite a hit indeed."

Hardly were they seated before they saw Miss

Vandevoort appear at the door, and stop to speak to the head waiter, who pointed to three or four tables; but Miss Vandevoort shook her head. She nodded carelessly to Mrs. Verry, and bowed more cordially to one or two others, but it was quite evident that she was searching for some one. It was also evident from the way her face lighted up, and a smile of recognition flashed over it, that it was Alice Copeland whom she was seeking, because she motioned to the head waiter, who bent himself double and preceded her, snapping his fingers at the other waiters, much as a ring-master cracks his whip at a horse which is doing the best it can already, for no especial reason except to call attention to his authority.

Arrived at the Copelands' table, she calmly seated herself next Alice in the chair reserved for Senator Cobb, giving the waiter to understand, in more ways than one, that it would be worth his while to obey her and to hold his tongue.

"If I were an artist I should paint you as Aurora, mademoiselle," said Judge Copeland. "Isn't she the radiant morning personified, daughter?"

"Oh, fie, Judge! You mustn't turn my head with your flattery."

"If I can only succeed in turning it in my direction, you place a premium on what you term flattery," answered the judge, gallantly.

Miss Vandevoort clapped her hands softly.

"How lovely!" she cried. "Judge Copeland, you put some of these unattached men to shame with the grace of your pretty speeches. Alice will have to go home and tell her mother that she saw Kate Vandevoort fall an easy victim to your blandishments."

Alice looked from one to the other. Such meaningless words, yet how different they seemed from other breakfast-table talk she could think of, and how excellently they raised everybody's spirits!

"How is your mother feeling on this fine day?"

Kate's brilliant face clouded over.

"Poor little Mamma! She is not well this morning, and I made her promise to lie still, and let me serve her breakfast later. She never eats the American breakfast, you know. And I like to carry her rolls and coffee to her myself. When she is ill, I am conceited enough to think that she likes it better if she takes it from me. There are only two of us left, you know, Judge, with John married, and the girls in Europe, and we have a little way of flattering each other by a great deal of petting, which, if we were all at home, would have to be scattered over the whole family. As it is, we concentrate it all on two. It is a sort of Liebig's Extract of Affection that we live on."

Waves of color came into her face as she talked of her mother, and softened it and made it even more lovely.

Alice was enchanted. She had been dazzled by Miss Vandevoort's brilliancy, but that one speech made it seem possible for her adoration to change into personal love, a much friendlier and more comfortable affair, as everybody knows who has tried both.

"Dear me, Alice, quickly! Watch the flamingo!"

"Flamingo!" said Alice. "Where is it?"

"I mean Mrs. Verry, my dear. There comes Senator Cobb, and he wants to come to this table, but she wants him there; that's why she took that table. I wonder if she will get him. Yes, she's landed him this time. No, he only stopped to speak. See how annoyed she looks. Oh, fie, Mrs. Verry, your natural color, when you are angry, does not harmonize with that you have put on out of your little box. Don't watch her so, my dear. It flatters her. Look into your plate and watch her through your eyelashes. Dear, dear, isn't she furious, and doesn't she hate us! Ah, good-morning, my dear Senator. Are you coming to our table? How very nice! See, you shall have this seat next to me, and I shall have the pleasure of handing you the fruit myself. How well you look this morning. Late hours do not seem to affect you in the least. Your freshness quite puts the rest of us to the blush."

The senator looked a little bewildered, but happy. He was at the age when, while he might have his preferences, flattery from any young woman upset him completely.

Miss Vandevoort's attentions to him during breakfast were really beautiful. She quite monopolized him, and pouted so frankly when he tried to talk across her to Alice that he was reduced to a powder of delight.

"Who is that beautiful woman?" asked Judge Copeland, as Miss Vandevoort bowed and kissed her fingers to a lady seating herself at the next table and facing them. She had snow-white hair, blue eyes, and the fresh, pink complexion of Alice herself.

"That is Mrs. Counselman," answered Kate, still smiling at her.

Alice's heart leaped, and she listened breathlessly for the next words.

"And that is her husband with her. Are they not a distinguished pair? Their son graduates this year, and a finer fellow never breathed. Mark my words, young Counselman will be heard from. I don't know why I say this, but I feel, whenever I am near him, that I am with the heart of a hero. His face follows me like the faces of some pictures in the Luxembourg. There is a haunting quality in it, which gives me a feeling that Destiny has already laid her hand upon his brow. It is foolish to allow one's thoughts to wander in that way, but I am glad the war is over. If it were not, he would lay down his life for some one, and perhaps nobody would ever hear of it. He might be shot carrying some wounded comrade from the field when the battle was all over. The heroism would be his, but not the glory."

Alice bit her lip and clenched her hands in her lap. She was afraid that she was going to cry before them all. What could Miss Vandevoort mean?

"His father is a most charming man. He got that sabre-cut at Gettysburg. He is a man of scholarly tastes and writes exquisite verse. To go into his library is to go into his life. But the Counselmans are a race of soldiers. His great-grandfather fought in the Revolution, and was killed at the battle of Brandywine. I shall say nothing of Mrs. Counselman. Her lovely face is her introduction to a man like yourself, Judge."

"Thank you, my dear. Will you do me the honor to present me to them after breakfast?"

"With much pleasure. Oh, what exquisite roses! Look, Alice."

Senator Cobb leaned back in his chair with a satisfied smile upon his face, as everybody turned to watch the head waiter coming down the room bearing a glorious bouquet of roses, which almost concealed him from view.

"They are for Miss Copeland," said the senator, rubbing his hands together.

Alice half rose from her chair in childish but indignant protest.

"Sit down," whispered Miss Vandevoort, twitching her dress under the table. But Kate frowned a trifle as she realized that there sat Mrs. Counselman, the mother of Gordon Counselman, who would see Alice receive so marked an attention from another. Kate's prehensile brain realized the subtlety of the situation. She knew that there was nothing like nipping these things in the bud.

"Oh, Senator Cobb!" she said, raising her voice a trifle. She reached out for the roses and they were placed in her hands. "Do let me give them to her," she murmured in the senator's ear.

"Certainly," he said, pleased at the sensation he had created, and delighted to see everybody craning their necks to watch Miss Vandevoort, with her face buried in the flowers, smiling and nodding at Senator Cobb, and apparently thanking him.

"Aren't they beautiful, Alice? And isn't the senator too kind and thoughtful for any use? But I feel dreadfully left out in the cold." She pretended to shiver, and looked reproachfully at the senator, who was so delighted at her raillery that he couldn't wash his hands fast enough. He stopped gurgling long enough to say,

"But, my dear young lady, just wait until dinner, and see what you will receive. You never know what a day may bring forth."

"With you around, that is quite true. You are like a fairy godfather, always dropping sugar-plums to your friends. But mind it is larger than this," she whispered, "or I shall be dreadfully jealous."

He nodded and chuckled and churned himself almost into hysteria with the intoxication of Miss Vandevoort's manner. It takes moral courage in a man to be true to one woman, if another woman has pitted her charms against him.

"These are yours, Alice dear. What shall I do with them?" said Miss Vandevoort, holding them towards her, but not offering to relinquish them. Alice drew back as if their odor sickened her.

"Oh, don't," she implored. "Keep them. Throw them away. Or no, wait a moment. Senator Cobb, are these flowers mine to do as I please with?"

"Certainly, my dear young lady. Certainly. Throw them away — throw them into the Hudson River, if you wish!" He chuckled again at this absurdity, and Miss Vandevoort coughed gently.

"Then I think I will send a few of them to your mother, Miss Vandevoort, if you think she would care for them. Mrs. Vandevoort is ill this morning, Senator Cobb."

Tears came into the senator's eyes at this exhibition of his lady-love's exquisite thoughtfulness. How little some men know the signs! If some one else had sent those roses, Mrs. Vandevoort might have had flowers sent to her, but they would not have been these.

In some way Kate Vandevoort walked out of the dining-room, at Senator Cobb's side, carrying Alice Copeland's flowers in her arms. And when presently she gave up guard-mounting, against the clamoring of a dozen importunate friends, in order to be with her mother at breakfast, she still had those flowers, all of which Alice had thrust upon her in a frenzy of gratitude.

VI

GUARD-MOUNTING

MANY people, of wide experience in other matters, absolutely deny the existence of love at first sight. They lay great stress upon the impossibility of such an occurrence, and point with pride to the fact that they are bank presidents, or treasurers of orphan asylums, or aldermen, to give weight to their opinions.

These facts silence, but do not convince. Men have been known to deny the possibility of a new world, and even while they were denying it most stridently some one who believed sailed away and found it, thus proving it beyond a peradventure. Just as, in the midst of these discussions, men and women are sailing away and discovering new worlds in each other's eyes, leaving those of us who are slow of heart to shut out the sight, if we are provincial, and loudly to declare that we do not believe in this new world because we have not sailed, and because we have not found it.

Be that as it may, Gordon Counselman, on that

eventful night when he looked down into Alice Copeland's blue eyes, felt his heart give an unmistakable leap under his tight gray coat, and something in his throat rose up and choked him and he could not speak for a moment, but stood looking down at her, alone with her for aught he saw or heard of others, and feeling that a girl who could look up at a fellow like that was enough to turn West Point back to the starting-place for all the world—the Garden of Eden—so called, perhaps, because two lovers were there alone with nobody to bother them or ask them to make up a set.

Young Counselman was no philosopher. He was simply a clean-minded fellow who fell in love as naturally and as gladly as only a chivalrous nature can, and who experienced as many pangs of unhappiness and doubt as always assail one in a first passion, but never with quite the same vernal poignancy as when it happens to come in one's youth, before one has had much time to note or discuss the symptoms in others. And not being a philosopher, he lived through these glories, frankly and unsuspiciously doing and saying the same things which millions of human beings had done before him, ingenuously believing that he was the first to discover just this delirious quality in the joy of love, betraying himself in a hundred little ways to any observant eyes, but utterly untormented by pagan doubts as to the genuineness or duration of this delightful state, such as occasionally will intrude themselves upon more experienced minds.

To those who are addicted to the unfortunate habit of analyzing, perhaps it is as sincere a test as any of the reality of a passion that one does believe one's self to be a pioneer in this line. And the fatuous questions lovers ask each other—whether any two people were ever so happy before, or if anybody ever loved with just the same largesse, or thought the same things, or felt such generous spasms of self-denial raging to be tested—prove even to the analytical that they are sailing over hitherto unknown waters towards the new world, which may not be just as their fancy painted it, but which is unmistakably strange and different, and at least brings the joy, at which even philosophers dare not cavil, of being the waking reality of all their inarticulate and half-formed dreams.

Of course Gordon Counselman did not discover all his capabilities in this direction during that first sleepless night when he thrashed around, wakeful, and confidently happy, ready to declare in the morning that he had not slept a wink, yet bearing in his radiant face the manifest signs of having been refreshed by what few lapses into unconsciousness he had been unable to take account of.

Twelve hours of being violently in love will teach

a man more of the subject than all the novels he ever read. And from being as heart-whole the evening before as ever a youth was, barring a few pangs laid to the account of Miss Kate Vandevoort, who had constantly to switch the attentions of the cadets from herself to younger girls, Gordon Counselman emerged from his quarters the next morning honestly feeling a year older and confident that he had run the whole gamut of human emotion from the lowest depth of bass despair to the highest treble of hope and faith. Cold gray daylight found him at neither extreme, but somewhere in the middle, with some uneasiness, some hope, and a great deal of determination. It is queer what a curious effect daylight has on love, and odd how many of the kinks the moon puts in that the sun takes out.

He was in such exuberant spirits, however, just to realize that she was here at West Point, breathing the same air, looking at the same river, treading the same ground, and that in an hour, perhaps half an hour, at almost any moment he might see her, that when he met Pratt, even though he knew Pratt wanted to borrow money, he hailed him with an enthusiasm of which Pratt was not slow to avail himself.

Gordon even allowed himself to be drawn into talk about it, although he had not a cent to lend, and really, except that his credit was good, was one of the most useless persons for Pratt to attempt. Gordon's kind heart, however, smote him for withholding his sympathy from so harassed a fellow as Pratt looked, and he thought perhaps if it were only a trifling scrape that he might see some way out of it.

Pratt realized the value of having at last got Counselman's ear, into which, to his honor be it said, no woes were ever poured in vain.

It was but a small thing in itself, only a question of a few hundred dollars; but to a cadet with no income of his own it was like the national debt would seem to a private citizen.

"But Pratt, old fellow, tell me how it came to be so much?" said Gordon, anxiously.

Pratt wriggled and colored, but finally, after one long look into Gordon's eyes, which had a trustworthiness in them which no one could mistake, thrust his hands between his knees and said with dogged determination :

"I'll tell you the whole thing, Counselman. I wasn't going to, but you've had the decency not to kick a fellow when he is down, and I'll just tell you. I got into debt over a woman—flowers and candy and truck. I'm in love with her. You needn't grin. You don't know what it is. But just you wait till some girl gets you in her clutches, and you'll be ready to sell your chevrons to get her a piece of the moon if she wants it. Mine is that kind. Other fellows give her the most expensive things and I've had to, or be left out of the race. I couldn't stand that, so I kept on till my credit was gone, and the governor shut down on me besides. Then I *was* in a hole. I've only been able to borrow small amounts of the other fellows, because I couldn't tell them this that I'm telling you, and when I paid some, of course they let me run those cursed bills a little higher. But long ago they stopped that and began hounding me besides. Now they are threatening to send them to the commandant. If they do, you know it's all up with me, and, by Jove! it will be the end of me too. I promise you that."

"What! Do you mean that you'd be such a coward as to wear a wooden overcoat if you don't graduate?"

"It isn't *that!*" cried Pratt, raising his head from his hands. "I'd lose the *girl!*"

"Oh," said Gordon. Then, "*I* haven't got any money."

"No," said Pratt, eagerly, "but you've got credit, and I have made all the arrangements. If you will just indorse my note they will take it, and I can take care of the interest."

"Why will they take my name instead of trusting you?"

"Why, you have kept your credit good and mine

is all knocked into smithereens. Anyhow, I asked them, and they said your name would be all right if you'd give it to me."

"Well, I'll do that, certainly, and be glad to. Of course it's only a guarantee that you will do your part, and I am not afraid that you won't."

"Counselman, you—you're the best fellow that I know, by Jove! And I'll never forget this as long as I live. You don't know what a load you have taken off my mind. I declare I could hardly breathe before. Now I can begin to enjoy her being here."

He wrung Gordon's hand twice.

"I'm going to marry her, Counselman, and I'd like you for best man. Will you?"

"Why, has it gone as far as that?" laughed Gordon.

"We are not engaged yet," admitted Pratt. "But she has given me to understand that she will marry me as soon as I graduate."

"I hope she won't miss the flowers."

"Oh, I can't stop sending them now! I've got to keep it up a little longer."

"Why, old man, are you in earnest? If you are thinking of marrying her, surely you are not going to add to your debts for your dowry."

"I've got to, if I keep in with her."

"Nonsense, old fellow. Just tell her you can't afford it. She will respect you for it, if she really cares for you."

"Well, *you* might be able to tell your girl if you had one, and it would go, but it's different with me, and different with Mrs. Verry."

"Mrs. Verry!" exclaimed Gordon.

"Certainly. What's the matter? Didn't you know who it was? I suppose you think it is queer that such a brilliant woman would condescend to marry a fellow like me. But she says she loves me, Counselman."

"Mrs. Verry!" repeated Gordon, as if unable to get it through his head. He wanted to say a dozen things, but it is rather difficult to look a fellow in the face and say that the woman he loves is years older than himself and that he believes her to be the worst kind of a flirt besides.

"It is not to be mentioned at present, Counselman. I have only told you."

"All right, old fellow. I—I'm really too surprised to say anything."

"I don't wonder," said Pratt, with unwonted humility.

When he was alone Gordon drew a long breath and shook his head. Then he put the matter out of his mind and went to hunt up George Copeland. He and George had been great friends, much to every one's surprise, but Gordon wanted to view him now in the new light of being Alice Copeland's brother. He sighed to think that if he had only known Alice sooner, what hours he could have spent asking George questions about her. He forgot that George probably would not have answered them. Brothers seldom are willing to sacrifice themselves to that extent, and George Copeland was unusually taciturn. Indeed, it was one of the problems of West Point why the most popular cadet there should have selected so cross-grained and quick-tempered a man for his best friend as George Copeland.

They really had not selected each other. It was one of those inevitable friendships among men which women never can understand.

Counselman was known to be set against fighting, and was a much respected arbitrator in many a subaltern disagreement. Added to this was the kindest heart in the world, which sometimes got him into trouble. He knew that his classmate Copeland's greatest fault, and an unforgivable fault at West Point, lay in attempting to take forty winks in the morning after the bugle sounded. Copeland had been reprimanded several times for being late, or for having something wrong with his attire—for what man can dress properly on a mad run? Counselman, not knowing George's surly temper, out of pure humanity once thrust his head in at the door of Copeland's quarters and roared out a warning, whereat George is said to have hurled a boot at Gordon's head. That is where he made a mistake, for in less time than one could wink, Gordon Counselman, the well-known peacemaker, had hauled George Copeland out of bed and was thrashing him roundly; and when he had all but knocked the breath out of George's astonished body, he politely invited him to dress and take the rest of what he had in for him.

But George, being wide awake by that time, cordially refused, and even apologized handsomely—partly for being thrashed and partly for so unamiably rewarding Gordon's brotherly act—after which, of course, they were the best of friends, and Gordon's authority as a peace-maker became more respected than ever.

But on this particular morning Gordon was not thinking of this incident, nor of the fact that George only showed his sullen temper nowadays after receiving a letter from his mother. If he had thought of them he would have dismissed all such unpleasant intruders—for Gordon's views of life were persistently rose-colored.

He could not find George, however, who was engaged in guard-mounting, but some girls found *him* and held him a prisoner for an anxious half-hour which he had meant to spend with Alice Copeland.

It really would be a delightful, as well as a most instructive thing, if a man occasionally could exchange places with the woman he loves and view his actions through her eyes. Perhaps he might better understand her causeless jealousies, her unreasonable way of holding him to account for quite harmless diversions. He might see how the moments he spends with other girls seem to lengthen into the basis of a quarrel—so different are men's eyes from women's. It would benefit them in the same degree that a year's travel benefits a provincial youth. He learns a new point of view.

Most men are provincial when they make love, but it is the provincialism of those who give the matter no thought, and not of bigotry.

When Miss Vandevoort took her radiant face and her brilliant flowers and her sweeping skirts from Alice's clinging view, the poor girl felt bereft. Nevertheless she crept close to her father and Mrs. Sheldon, the commandant's wife, and went with them to witness guard-mounting with a beating heart.

The martial spirit in her leaped out to meet the boys in gray as they marched towards her, every eye to the front, every step taken with such clocklike precision that it made her dizzy to watch them. In vain she looked for Gordon Counselman. The brown faces under their shakoes all looked alike to her, and she was sure if he had been among them he would have looked different. The adjutant, covered with gold lace, made a brave showing; but still he was not the one she sought. Nevertheless there were moments when the impressive spectacle before her drew her thoughts from him, and left no room for anything except the majesty of the military; for when, at the last, the old Officer of the Day turns the detail over to the new Officer of the Day, and, making the salute—the most stately, the most impressive of all—by removing his helmet and holding it with matchless dignity to his left shoulder, so stands with bared head while he passes out of office, Alice felt that it was worth while being Officer of the Day just for the majestic manner in which he was permitted to resign the office.

Hardly, however, had the band struck up " The Girl I Left Behind Me," and the detail marched away, when she saw Gordon Counselman in a group of girls who seemed to be literally besieging him.

It is one of the unanswered conundrums of life why the anger of a lover rises to a white-heat at a similar display of his own mild insanity in any one else. Alice instantly set those girls down as bold and forward and unladylike ; and many more such adjectives did she heap upon them in the secret recesses of a heart which never before had known a pang of jealousy in all its gentle existence. She was partly consoled, however, by the unmistakable way in which his brown face flushed when he saw her. She even gave him credit for an effort to detach himself from the tenacious girls who surrounded him, for she distinctly saw him bow and endeavor to withdraw; but they made such a little laughing clamor over him, and coaxed him so prettily, and he was so evidently their hero as well as hers, that a little sick thrill ran through her, and a film came over the beauty of the scene, and she turned to look for her father, and wanted to go back to Stockbridge where she couldn't see him, or, at least, where she couldn't see him with other girls.

But her father was not there and Senator Cobb was. He was making for her too. But bearing down upon him like a revenue cutter was Mrs. Verry. Alice smiled a wintry little smile of amusement. Thanks to Miss Vandevoort's tutelage she was beginning to see below the surface, and it looked to her like a human game of hare and hounds.

She never knew the load of unhappiness that settled down upon Gordon Counselman as he saw the rich senator from Ohio so palpably appropriating Alice, and dampening the ardor which had been surging up in his heart at the sight of her to the verge of bursting off some of his shining buttons, as Peggotty was wont to shed hers under sudden effervescence of affection.

So those two foolish young people looked across at each other and allowed the wrong people to monopolize them, and were frankly and honestly miserable over the perversity of fate or their own stupidity in not rising to the occasion. When, finally, young Counselman made a dash for liberty, and asked her to walk down old Flirtation with him in his only hour of leisure, Alice said to him:

"I've promised to go with Senator Cobb," in such a woebegone tone, and with such a glance of aversion at the poor senator, that Gordon was comforted a little in spite of his bitter disappointment.

"Stay and talk to me just a moment," he urged, frankly turning his back on the senator and his claims.

She colored so prettily with pleasure that Gordon was sure she would; but just then her father said:

"Come, daughter, Mrs. Sheldon wishes to go;" and with only one backward glance full of acquiescence and longing to accept, Alice was sandwiched between the unsuspicious Mrs. Sheldon and her father, and taken back to the hotel, where, waiting for them, she found Kate Vandevoort.

Alice mentally flung herself upon Miss Vandevoort's mercy and into her arms, telling her secret quite unsuspiciously with the desperate words:

"I promised to go to walk with Senator Cobb, and just afterwards, when it was too late, Mr. Counselman asked me."

Miss Vandevoort wrinkled her smooth brow in vexation for a moment, then she threw back her head and laughed her old laugh of amusement at the ways of people.

"Why do you laugh?" asked Alice.

"Because if I didn't, I should weep. Laughing keeps me on the surface. But don't look so wretched, my dear." She took Alice's flushed cheeks between her thumb and forefinger very daintily. "Let me see if we cannot think of an antidote."

"How good you are," murmured Alice. "I thought you would be vexed at my stupidity. I'm such a little fool," she ended, with vicious emphasis.

"I am glad you are beginning to realize it," said Miss Vandevoort, with amazing coolness. "It is the first step towards reform. What made you promise to go with Senator Cobb?"

"It came so suddenly. I had no excuse ready."

"Why didn't you say you had an engagement?"

"Because it wouldn't have been the truth," said Alice, with the unconscious rudeness of conscious virtue.

"*Ciel!*" said Miss Vandevoort under her breath. "What a long way Stockbridge is from New York. Millions and millions of miles. Don't look so mystified, child. Whenever you are puzzled, nod your head with an air of intelligence calculated to deceive even the elect. Then keep your ears open and the gullible elect will straightway tell you all there is to know about it. When you are unhappy, laugh. Laugh out loud, show all your teeth—you have very pretty teeth and you can afford to laugh even at poor jests. When you are with your sweetheart, don't smile and look contented and happy. If you do, some jealous girl will get him away from you. Look droopy and bored, so that people will not envy you. You are a shining mark, my dear, with that face of yours such a map of your emotions. If you can't do anything else, look stupid. I wonder if you could—with those eyes? It is invaluable to be able to look stupid. It disarms everybody. I always am so sorry for people with really intellectual faces—people with long, scholarly features, who can only control their expression. They always are obliged to take the credit for what they know, and they are doomed to be feared by the very ones they care most to attract. Now I am different. Let me tell you a secret. My face is my fortune because it does not betray me. I can look like a perfect fool, a puppet, the tool of any designing man or woman. Look at me now. Do I look as if I could spell 'necessary' and 'separate'? Shouldn't you think that I would spell 'believe' and 'receive' alike, and that I should much prefer to take my views on life from my husband? That is why I have such a good time. I am clever and nobody knows it. Promise not to betray my secret."

Miss Vandevoort said this with such an engaging air, and with so whimsical an expression, that Alice was ready to declare that she was the funniest as well as the most fascinating woman she ever had met, which, considering her narrow experience, was hardly as great a compliment as she meant it to be.

"But to return to Senator Cobb. Much as I should dislike to be the first one to set your feet in the downward path, I wish I could teach you not to be quite so hopelessly truthful. Why, what's the matter? I only mean that it is not necessary to tell all you think in order to believe yourself honest. Tactlessness is not a virtue even if the ignorant do dub it honesty. It is a downright crime. I wish I could teach you to veil the truth with illusion—pure white illusion—because the naked truth is shocking to the scrupulously modest. Now, I am clever enough to know that I never can teach you to do this well, and unless you can do it well it is much better to leave it alone and just vulgarly to tell the truth, the whole truth, and nothing but the truth, and let people hate you, as they surely will. Nobody wants undiluted honesty, least of all, men. But the mistake women make is in coloring the truth. They make it gray, and gray is dull and unbecoming. Now when *I* color the truth I make it red. Most men love red. It warms and cheers, and my little pink and rose colored lies are among my greatest charms. Why, my dear Alice, if I had told the brutal truth to unattractive men all my life, I should be literally nowhere. I should have been laid on the shelf long ago."

"Yes, but," said Alice, flushing and laughing, "there was nothing to do about Senator Cobb except to say, 'I don't want to go with you,' and have it really true."

"Well, why didn't you say that?"

"Because it would have hurt his feelings."

"Precisely. I am glad to see that you do not want to hurt even Senator Cobb's feelings. From the way you started to walk right across the breakfast-table this morning in order to get rid of him, I was afraid you were capable of anything. Never hurt any man's feelings. He never forgets it. You took the other horn of the dilemma and made yourself wretched. I have always thought of the Dilemma as a horned sphinx. Now I am too selfish to impale myself on either horn. I avoid both and seat myself calmly between them on her brow, where I remain like a diadem. All my life I have been dodging bores and landing clever men and floating in to shore on the high tide of success without letting anybody catch me at my harmless little tricks except other women. I wouldn't let them if I could have helped myself. But other women are sometimes too much for me. I never wound a man's vanity. Believe me, Alice, it is the best, the *only* safe way. Now make a *bona fide* engagement with me to spend every spare moment with me which you do not care to spend elsewhere. Do you promise? Well, now you can truthfully say, ' I have another engagement.' "

As Miss Vandevoort ceased speaking she watched Alice wistfully, as though the absolute truthfulness of the girl appealed to her in a very tender way, yet she mentally stamped it impossible. Miss Vandevoort's heart and intellect generally warred in this way.

" But you haven't told me what to do," said Alice.

" Oh no. Well, let me think."

She laid a finger on her lips, and, leaning forward, stood looking at the toe of her little shoe with serious attention; and unconsciously Alice, as most absorbed persons do, followed her example, looking down and regarding it with equal heed. Presently a light broke over Miss Vandevoort's face and she threw back her head.

" I have it," she said. "Ask no questions, but put on your prettiest frock, the one which fits the best in the back. All your gowns should fit best in the back, for your back is at the mercy of the observer. You can defend the front in fifty ways, but how do you know what is going on behind you?

A woman of genius has the backs of her gowns faultless. Mine are! The fronts of mine are plain. You never notice them, because I myself am the front of a gown. Now listen. Wear your prettiest and go with him. Keep your wits about you and trust the rest to me."

"I will, I truly will!" said Alice, impetuously. She stood looking up into Miss Vandevoort's smiling, whimsical, magnetic face with the dilated gaze of a fascinated child. Miss Vandevoort had captured her imagination, and opened vistas in her own life, down which she looked with a breathless thrill. The possibilities seemed so great. Perhaps it was only one way Miss Vandevoort had of exercising her cleverness, so lightly to talk with Alice as to banish her depression and nerve her for her difficult talk. In this she had succeeded at any rate. Alice's eyes of faith made her own almost wistful again.

"I believe," breathed Alice fervently, in a swift, exultant comprehension of her changed spirits, "that you could almost raise the dead, you are so wonderful and so much alive!"

It was but an idle form of speech, a childish exaggeration; but her smile froze as she saw the horror in Miss Vandevoort's face. Even her brilliant scarlet lips grew pale under Alice's stricken gaze.

"Oh, what *have* I said?" cried Alice, springing towards her and seizing her hand.

"Nothing. It is nothing. Only my heart. It troubles me at times," gasped Miss Vandevoort, recovering herself with a visible effort. She rubbed her cheeks with both hands as if she realized their whiteness.

Alice watched the color creep back into her face, and Miss Vandevoort bore her anxious gaze unflinchingly and smiled bravely. And it was only after Alice, entirely reassured, had left her, that Kate Vandevoort turned away, out of the sight of everybody, and covered her trembling lips with her hands to keep down a bitter cry, murmuring brokenly,

"Raise the dead, did she say? O God, dear God, if I only could!"

VII

DOWN FLIRTATION WALK

"I WONDER," said Miss Vandevoort to herself as she came out of the hotel on the veranda and began idly to pace its length, apparently absorbed in putting on her gloves, but in reality doing sentry duty, "if it can be possible that these two young creatures are going to care for each other, or am I deceived in the signs? If they were like other people—if Gordon were as selfish as other young fellows—or if Alice were as frivolous as other girls, I might think this were only a passing attraction; but they are both so true. Heavens, how it brings it all back! How will it end with them? They are both so young and so unworldly. How hard it will go with either, if the other is not seriously interested. I could easily bring myself to believe in both of them if it did not seem too good to be true—and good things of the heart come so seldom in this world. Gordon is too popular. If it is possible to spoil him these girls will do it. Ah, bless the boy!

I can't blame them. He is the delight of my eyes. But if I let him know it, I shall be just as unwise as they. I really pity these wonderfully attractive men, with such a natural, irresistible charm as Gordon has. The poor fellows have no chance to be modest and chivalrous. It is all our fault. Dear me, I wonder if that difficult young person— Miss Alice Copeland, who dislikes young men—has any idea of what a dear fellow Gordon is. Well, I must see what I can do to stir things up. I can be very annoying when I try. How do you do, Mr. Counselman? Am I not a wonder to be ready ahead of time and actually waiting for so punctual a person as yourself?"

"How lovely you look, Miss Vandevoort!" exclaimed the boy, looking at her out of his smiling eyes with such frank admiration that she colored.

"Oh, Gordon, you are impossible. There is no use trying to reform you. Your honesty is so believable, and that is dangerous, even to a case-hardened person like myself. I really catch myself *trying* to look well for you! Now isn't that a dreadful admission, when I had just determined never to say another thing to spoil you?"

Gordon pulled off his shako and laughed such a boyish, hearty laugh that two old ladies turned their heads and smiled at him. Alice Copeland heard it, coming out of the parlor with Senator

Cobb, and she took an involuntary step forward, thereby losing what the senator was saying, and having to listen to it all over again.

What girl at a summer resort has not felt the misery of coming out on the veranda with the wrong man, only to see the right man with another girl? And if the other girl was having her glove buttoned at just that particular moment, as Kate was, and your own soul's property was bending over her hand—actually holding it, as everybody knows a man has to do when he buttons a glove—and if the other girl was so absorbed in the interesting process that she did not look up to bow, or give him a chance to bow, and you had to go on down the steps, chattering to this other man, who suddenly has become so hateful to you that you almost wished he would trip on the steps and land on his head—then you can truthfully say that you know what real misery is.

Kate felt a pang of sympathy for Alice as she caught her imploring look and steadfastly "for the sake of the future" refused to answer it. And she saw with genuine admiration the plucky way that Alice gathered herself together and held her head high and chatted with the senator.

"Ah, there goes Alice Copeland," said Kate, calmly.

"Where, where?" asked Gordon, dropping her

hand and looking in all directions except the right one.

"Why, down there. See?"

"Then come on," said Gordon, eagerly, picking up his helmet and straightening himself.

"Come where?" asked Miss Vandevoort, innocently. "Are you going to follow them?"

"Why no, of course not," he answered, awkwardly. "Only you said—"

"I said that *I* would walk with you if you liked. Alice has an escort. Look how well she carries herself. Dear me, how devoted the senator seems. I wonder if she would marry him. Her mother would favor it heart, soul, influence, and will power. To see her child a social power in Washington. Dear, dear, how well she would like it. Did you ever see Mrs. Copeland, Gordon?"

"No."

"Ever see a picture of her?"

"No."

"Well, if you ever see her, look at her nose. The history of the Copeland family is written in the shape of Mrs. Copeland's nose. My dear boy, if Napoleon could have seen it, he would have made her a field-marshal."

"Isn't Senator Cobb very rich?" asked Gordon, presently, with his brows drawn into a straight line.

"I believe so. But the Copelands are richer."

"Then perhaps Mrs. Copeland would not favor him as a suitor on that ground."

"It is power she covets, not wealth. Stern blue Presbyterian that she is, she hankers after the flesh-pots of Egypt. She would like to have the judge in the Cabinet, only he will not enter politics—grand old gentleman that he is—and how she would revel in the social despotism that would be hers."

Kate watched him narrowly as she said these things. He looked after Alice's retreating figure wistfully a moment, then squared his shoulders, and the sunny look came back into his eyes, as he said:

"If Alice Copeland is the girl I take her to be, she will marry the man she *loves*."

"Come on," said Kate, gayly. "I am ready now. Suppose we walk down old Flirtation."

"Why, we must have walked faster than they, for here we are almost upon them," she said in her most guileless manner, ten minutes later.

Gordon looked down at her quizzically, but she looked back at him with such innocence that he laughed aloud, and Alice turned around and smiled at them.

"Wait for us!" cried Kate, swinging her parasol at them.

"What a darling you are!" whispered Gordon, audaciously.

"How disrespectful of you," said Kate. "What do you mean?"

She looked so surprised that Gordon was abashed. He was so honest himself that Miss Vandevoort's brilliant changes of base always nonplussed him. But that astute young woman had no intention of openly championing his cause until she felt her ground secure beneath her feet.

"Senator Cobb," she said, when they all four stopped to speak, "do you remember what I was telling you in Washington last month about Mrs. Frederick's flirtation with Captain Connor of the navy?"

"Yes, yes, I remember," said the senator, eagerly, who dearly loved a bit of gossip.

"Well, I know the rest of it now. Some time I'll tell you, if you promise solemnly not to repeat it. But I wonder if I can trust you?"

"Oh, indeed you can, my dear lady. I never speak of such things. Was it as we thought?"

"Never mind now. I must not intrude upon your walk with Miss Copeland. I'll tell you some time when you come up to New York."

"Oh, I never can wait that long. Tell me now. Perhaps Miss Copeland will walk with Mr. Counselman for a minute or two."

"Well, come on, then. Leave them to follow. But mind you never breathe this."

And so for a blissful thirty minutes Gordon Counselman and Alice followed in the wake of a bald head and a bronze head which were so close together that when they met Mrs. Verry and Pratt, Mrs. Verry was guilty of the indiscretion of turning to look after them.

Miss Vandevoort made such good use of her time with the senator from Ohio that he walked all the way back with her, and Alice only joined them when Gordon dashed away to take part in dress-parade.

Seldom does the parade-ground present so brilliant a sight as during graduation week, when hosts of visitors and pretty girls and proud relatives are gathered there to do homage to the most beautiful sight in the world—a perfectly trained battalion on a perfect parade-ground.

The Board of Visitors was unusually imposing this year, and the array of beautiful girls unusually attractive; but Alice, from the moment she saw that parade form, forgot everything except that all those men, with their apparently perfect uniforms and shining equipments and faultless appearance, were not so perfect or so faultless as Gordon, for he, her hero, was first captain of them all.

It was an impressive sight. The visitors made a bright spot of color in front of the officers' quarters, with the old gray academy buildings looming up on one side, while away off at the other the grim barracks were aligned, in front of which the companies were forming. The lovely Hudson flowed softly beneath the bluff, visible beyond the Point like a curving band of silver. The sunlight slanted across the smooth parade-ground, glimmering on company after company of cadets in full-dress uniforms, being marched up from their quarters by proud cadet officers, who endeavored to look as if all this fuss-and-feathers was a good deal of a bore to full-grown men, and never knowing that their ingenuous young countenances hopelessly betrayed the fact that they loved every unnecessary inch of red tape, and that they wouldn't have exchanged places with civilians in dun-colored tweeds for all that this world had to offer.

The advancing column halted at a word, as motionless as statues. Alice could see Gordon in the post of honor at the extreme right. He was the first to step forward with a command to his company. All the other cadet captains had to follow *him*. Then the band marched out, as if to show *them*selves, and paraded down the front of the column and back again, as much as to say, " Now, boys, watch us. This is the way you want to march." How the girls loved that band! They never could make up their minds which to prefer, the bearskin of the drum-major or the gold-lace of the adjutant, who, just as soon as the band got back to their places, gave a hoarse command, which nobody understood, because that would have been unmilitary. Everybody obeyed it, however, because the ranks opened and all the officers marched forward in front of their companies and halted.

Again the adjutant gave a hoarse cough, and all the long column presented arms as if pulled by one string, while the officers saluted. Then came the adjutant's turn to subside for a while. Having done all that could reasonably be expected of one man, he wheeled, saluted the commandant, and said, in a more conversational tone, "Sir, the parade is formed." At least the girls heard that. Two or three of the liveliest mimicked his salute and touched their big leghorn hats with their hands. It annoyed Alice. She thought it disrespectful, not to say sacrilegious. She wished Gordon had been nearer, so that she could see his face.

The adjutant was at his post, and the commandant was putting the men through a drill all too short to satisfy the voracious admiration of the girls, who wished he had left them there indefinitely. The stupid part of dress-parade to women is where they receive reports and instructions. Everybody talks during this time. But when the order came "Parade is dismissed," and the adjutant took his place in the centre of the line of officers, who closed in upon him in front of the battalion, forming a small and exclusive column, Gordon, as first captain, still at the right, a sharp word of command came from the adjutant himself, and then, oh, then the column of officers, with the band blowing itself red in the face, marched up, up, up, like beautiful, live, human machines, towards the commandant, standing in rigid and solitary dignity, and towards the visitors, who applauded them mightily, and towards the girls, who leaned forward with eyes blazing with excitement and cheeks aflame with delight. Alice felt her heart almost turn over with pride and gratitude and love, and even Kate Vandevoort's eyes swam in tears of sympathy as she squeezed the hand Alice had impetuously thrust into hers.

Ah, it was a brave sight, and all too soon over. It was beautiful to see how carelessly the cadet officers strolled up afterwards to mingle with the visitors and to parry the enthusiasm of fond mothers and lively girls, with a fine disregard of their eager compliments, but an ear greedy for more of the same thing.

George Copeland began to open his eyes when he saw what a centre of attraction his sister had become. He was bored to death by cadets begging to be introduced, and to his disgust he found that whenever he wanted Counselman, it would be better and simpler just to look for Alice. He never had thought her pretty in Stockbridge. In fact, he never had thought of her at all, except when he wanted her to wait on him, for her willing feet flew on his errands as ungrudgingly as on her mother's. But here she was so pretty that he was surprised.

He went up to his father and handed him a letter.

"Here is a letter for sister, sir, which came in one of mine," he said.

"From whom, son?"

"From mother," he answered, his face darkening involuntarily.

"What did she have to say? How is she?"

"Here it is. I haven't read it, sir. I—I haven't had time," he stammered, in answer to his father's quick glance.

"Thank you, son," said Judge Copeland, putting the letter in his pocket. He fingered the one addressed to Alice uncertainly, and looked affectionately at her bright face, where the color was fluttering as he never had seen it before. He looked down at the letter again, then sighed and put it with the other. He did not realize that George was watching him.

"That's right," muttered George, turning away. "No use in spoiling the child's pleasure now. I'll bet the governor doesn't read mine in a hurry for all he's so polite about it." He scowled as he thought of the pile in his quarters, unopened and unanswered, into which his mother had poured a great deal of mother love in spite of being so mixed up with the bulletins of the sick in Stockbridge, and advice about his own health—that no one but Job or a woman could have stood it to read them.

Gordon was one of the managers of the hop, and had to tear himself away early, leaving Alice an opportunity to be very quiet as she walked back to the hotel with Miss Vandevoort and Senator Cobb.

The only thing she remembered about dinner was being very much amused at an enormous bouquet of yellow roses that Senator Cobb had caused to be sent to Miss Vandevoort, as a result of that charming young lady's coquetry of the morning. Then there was a breathless hour in which she dressed herself for the hop—eager, nay, anxious almost to the verge of tears, to be lovely just that one night for Gordon Counselman's sake. No need for Kate Vandevoort to advise her to wear her very prettiest frock or to look more animated, Her nervousness flushed her cheeks and made her great eyes black, so that when Miss Vandevoort rapped smartly on Alice's door and came in to inspect her costume and to urge her to take herself well in hand, instead of the shy, timid little maid from Stockbridge she had expected to see, she was confronted by a radiant creature with eyes like stars, who held her head high and challenged your best admiration on the spot.

"*Mon Dieu!*" cried Miss Vandevoort. "Where is the little Alice Copeland I came to see? I am looking for a little mouse of a girl, whose hair I was to tidy and whose tucker I was to smooth, and who was going to creep into my pocket and only poke her head out for George to dance with twice and for her father to take into supper. Where is she?"

"Oh," laughed Alice, clasping her hands together in delight, "am I so different? I feel different, Miss Vandevoort. I never felt this way before. I have always hated to dance, but to-night I hope that I shall be asked often. I can hardly wait to begin."

Miss Vandevoort reached out for support in a surprise which was not feigned.

"Alice," she said, weakly, "you'll be the death of me. Your Quaker attitude of yesterday contrasted with your *fin de siècle* attitude of to-day is too much for my feeble brain to grasp. I never realized the magic of old Flirtation before."

"It wasn't that—" began Alice, hastily. But Kate held up her hand.

"Don't add the sin of falsehood to your other crimes, Alice," she said, solemnly.

"What other crimes?" asked Alice.

"The crime of deceiving me. I thought you were

a little brown wren. I find you a bird-of-paradise. Come on! I hear the band. We mustn't miss a moment to-night! As a rule I make a triumphant entry late, looking cool and fresh when the other girls are warm and a trifle dishevelled from a waltz; but to-night I want to be early and sit in the bald-headed row and see the curtain go up. Here is your fan. Tuck your handkerchief in there. Where are your hair-pins? I want just one to fasten this curl. Now, I think you are perfect. Who sent these flowers—Senator Cobb?"

"No. Mr.—Mr. C—Counselman sent them," stammered Alice with flaming cheeks.

Miss Vandevoort turned her head away and bit her lips. Not for worlds would she have had Alice see her smile.

"They are very handsome," she said. "That looks like a bouquet that Gordon Counselman would send. Pink roses and lilies-of-the-valley. I really think that is the most beautiful and appropriate bouquet I ever saw."

"Do you, really?" cried Alice. "I thought so, but I didn't expect everybody to agree with me."

"I do, at any rate, and I am a judge. You can tell quite a good deal about a man by the kind of flowers he sends you."

"Then Senator Cobb must be very artistic," said Alice, laughing.

"Senator Cobb has an artistic florist. He never designates what kind of flowers shall be sent. Gordon does. Now hold your dress up on both sides—a little more on the left—and come with me."

Judge Copeland, Senator Cobb, and George Copeland were waiting for them, and as soon as they appeared at the door of the hop-room, Gordon Counselman was with them instantly, looking past all the other girls—past even lovely Kate Vandevoort herself—to Alice, who never looked so pretty nor so sweet as when she laid her hand shyly on Gordon's arm and paused to look at the decorations, all of which, though he would not say so, were his taste.

No one could deny that the room was beautiful, for the military lends itself readily to decorations. From crossed sabres and stacked arms up to small cannon, everywhere were the signs of the peaceful side of war; and over and under and above, in all kinds of soft draperies and flowing festoons, the flag—the dear, dear flag—that flag which taste and love and patriotism all combine to make us think the most beautiful in the world; the flag which pulls at your heartstrings like a human thing when you see it floating anywhere; which makes you want to put your hand on it and love it if you see pictures of it with hosts of others; which, when you accidentally run across it in Europe, makes you want to kiss and hug and cry over it, if you are a woman, and stand up and take your hat off to it, if you are a man.

Gordon watched Alice as her eyes fell upon these flags. She looked up at him without speaking, and he pressed the hand which lay on his arm against his tight gray coat, and, perhaps, she closed her fingers a little more closely on his sleeve: but of that no one can be sure. At any rate, they understood each other without words, as we are told lovers have a little way of doing, so that when Gordon said "I love it," Alice said "So do I," and each knew that the other meant the flag.

Who shall describe a girl's first ball, with plenty of partners and her dress satisfactory and the floor good and the band military, and the man of her heart the superb dancer that Gordon Counselman was?

Gordon danced with just the same generous enthusiasm and out-of-door swing that he put into his riding and his swimming. It was whole-hearted and athletic and elastic, and people always watched him and felt the younger for it, and asked who he was.

George came up after Alice's card was filled and asked to see it. He hated to dance, but it was something to step into a ring of 'the other fellows" crowding around a girl, and to call her by her Christian name, and to pat her hand with an air of proprietorship which made "the other fellows" greei with envy.

"Why, your card is all filled," he said, in a tone of disappointment. Alice was so surprised that he really showed some feeling, and so grateful and so touched, that she almost stammered in her eagerness to explain.

"No, George, I saved one for you. This one with the cross over it. That is for you. I saved it. I thought perhaps you would be late asking me."

There was no reproach in her honest little soft voice, and it was sisterly affection and gratitude for his notice which flushed her cheeks in such a bewitching manner that Gordon Counselman was obliged to turn away for fear "the other fellows" would see how he felt about her. "The other fellows" are both the Mrs. Grundy and the Sir Hubert of West Point.

Alice Copeland's evening, if one might judge by her radiant face, possessed no drawbacks, even in spite of Gordon's undoubted popularity with buds, young ladies, and even old ladies, who *would* stop him, to pat his arm and ask how he was enjoying himself, when he was dashing from one partner to another.

Perhaps his unfortunate experience of the morning had taught him a lesson in the despatch necessary to exercise with a popular girl, for in that walk down old Flirtation, he had mapped out the dances he wanted with Alice, and she had given them to him with such shy, happy eyes that the impetuous young cadet wanted to tell her right then and there that he loved her with all his boyish heart and soul, and perhaps Alice wouldn't have been so very angry if he had.

Miss Vandevoort stopped in at Alice's room, after it was over, to talk about it.

"Did you have a good time, dearie?"

"Oh, *so* good!" cried Alice, clasping her hands. "I do believe I am the happiest girl in the world. Everything is so beautiful, isn't it?"

"Yes, everything. And I have the most beautiful news of all to tell you now."

"Oh, what is it? How could anything be lovelier than to-night has been?"

"Well, your brother has invited Gordon Counselman to spend part of his leave at your house, and perhaps Mollie Overshine will ask me down to Stockbridge for the same time."

"Oh, dear Miss Vandevoort!"

Alice could say no more. She wanted to say so much, but something came up in her throat and choked her. Perhaps it was her own great happiness. Perhaps it was a something in Kate Vandevoort's wistful, smiling eyes. But whatever it was, when Kate made a little impetuous movement

of her arms as if to open them, Alice sprang forward
and flung herself into them, hiding her face in the
laces on Kate's breast, and clinging to her dumbly
as if knowing that she understood because she was
a woman. And while they stood thus, a voice from
below, which they both recognized as Gordon Counselman's, began to sing the first verse of that dear
old song, " Benny Havens, O," and instantly voice
after voice caught it up, until the cadets were ser-
enading the girls at the hotel with, save and except-
ing " Fair Harvard," the most musical, the most
pathetic, the most haunting college melody ever
sung by human throats:

> "Fill up your glasses, fellows,
>   And stand up in a row,
> To sentimental drinking we
>   Are going for to go.
> In the army of sobriety,
>   Promotion's rather slow,
> We'll sigh o'er reminiscences
>   Of Benny Havens, O!"

As these words rang clearly out upon the quiet
night, Alice felt the sudden clutch of Kate's arms
around her, and Kate bent her tall head and laid
her cheek on Alice's soft hair a moment, and a sob
rose in her throat that Alice could not help but
hear — oh, the memories of old songs! — then she
put the girl gently away from her and went out,

still without speaking. Perhaps she could not bear to have Alice see her face.

When she had gone, Alice went and knelt down by the open window and listened to the fresh young voices which floated the music up to her as if on wings, and it all seemed so beautiful and so sad, and she was young and so much in love that she began to cry very softly, as if she, too, had memories which the dear song waked to life—only she hadn't. But it never does women any harm to weep and sob and cry their hearts out over tender, old-fashioned music. And if they were not just that gentle and sentimental and soft-hearted, the men would never love them as they do.

VIII

COUNTER-IRRITANTS

MRS. COPELAND so seldom indorsed anybody whom the family liked that it was quite a pleasant surprise to them when she metaphorically took Kate Vandevoort to her bosom and made it evident by her thawed manner that the Vandevoorts' ancestry equalled the Copelands'. Furthermore, and in addition to this fundamental fact, Kate was a stupendous social success, the belle of three cities. This, too, had its weight.

An idol of the people is on so insecure a footing that it behooves one who aspires to that slippery elevation to look well to what sort of a cushion is beneath him, unless he likewise aspires to broken bones and bruised feelings, for, by a single "Thumbs down," he is apt to find himself shaken up, out of breath and dizzy from his fall.

A social idol, a belle, is perhaps in the most precarious situation of all, and this made the triumphal march of Miss Vandevoort all the more surprising, inasmuch as she conquered everything and everybody, wherever she chose, and did it apparently without effort. It was not that she was so beautiful—hosts of buds came on the scene of action whose features were more regular than hers. It was not because she had family and great wealth at her back; many girls have failed to become belles who have had both. Nor could it be laid entirely to her personal magnetism, although it could not fail of being a somewhat potent factor when it was sufficient to win over and hold some who openly avowed enmity before coming in range of her electricity. Perhaps more than all, but in conjunction with these necessary attractions, it was her absolutely sincere interest in the lives of other people, which never fails to fascinate, and her sense of humor, that gift of the gods, who show how little they value women by their niggardliness towards them with this celestial gift. We women have a right to question the wisdom of Olympus, when we, who must of necessity cope with the petty, narrow, hateful woman-worries of life, are only given the shield of Patience and are denied the buckler of Humor, when we might just as well have had both and been invulnerable, all but the heel.

Tito Melema maintained his popularity by pretending to give the honor to another, always another, and apparently keeping himself in the background, which cunning policy served to keep him the idol of the people until they discovered that they were being tricked.

Although Miss Vandevoort was just the one to appreciate the cleverness of Tito, she was far too impatient of the restrictions which any set policy imposed to bind herself to anything which threatened to fetter her freedom to be individual and natural. The whimsical theories which she expounded to Alice Copeland she lived up to truly, yet only because her nature, in spite of her free speech, was of the kindliest, and because it was natural to her to wish to please.

Thus, when she turned her amused eyes on one who mentioned her popularity in her presence, he at once felt that she, too, was but an interested spectator at the show, and that she held it at its proper value, even scorning what might so easily be lost. She mocked and laughed at the idea that people seriously discussed the fact that she was a belle, and held them and herself and all such up to such sincere ridicule that they were compelled, much against their will, half-way to believe her. In consequence they, too, turned around and gave her the homage which she seemed to value so lightly, and which, with the true amiability of human nature, they so gladly would have withheld had they felt that she depended upon it.

Mrs. Copeland reverenced Power; perhaps because circumstances, Fate, Destiny, what you will, had denied her the exercise of it, save in a small way, she reverenced Social Power more than all.

Not through the Overshines alone, but in countless ways—through travellers who had met her abroad, through the vulgar channels of the daily newspapers, which Mrs. Copeland openly denounced, and read in private, and through her hosts of friends in Philadelphia and New York who knew Kate—did Mrs. Copeland become conversant with her social successes. So when this young goddess signified her willingness not only to pay her cousin Mollie Overshine a visit, but to meet and mingle with Stockbridge society, a thing which she never had done before, the secret delight of several first families almost burst their good Quaker bounds. However much the people living there might discuss their chronic ill-health and deprecate the unbroken quiet of Stockbridge, they sincerely objected to having a New York belle frankly declare that hitherto she had used their town simply as a sanitarium.

When she arrived Mrs. Copeland at once called upon her, and invited the Overshines and Miss Vandevoort to dine, changing her dinner-hour, as she did upon state occasions, from noon to seven o'clock, for the accommodation of their honored guest.

Kate arrayed herself with unusual care for that dinner at the Copelands, and she was quite thoughtful for several hours beforehand. Her casual acquaintance with Mrs. Copeland, supplemented by Mollie Overshine's shrewd anecdotes, had taught her that here was a foeman worthy of her steel—a woman who would unflinchingly sacrifice her daughter's happiness to her own ambition. In meeting her again, she felt that peculiar antagonized feeling to which impressionable natures are so sensitive. You can only explain this to one who is in the habit of experiencing it. Mrs. Copeland never would have understood it. She had no intuitions, and she often thanked Heaven that she was not sensitive.

As Kate swept into the Copeland drawing-room in an evening dress so extreme that it looked as if it were slipping from her polished shoulders, Mrs. Copeland simply closed her eyes. But she opened them again when she remembered that it was Miss Vandevoort who wore it.

Kate possessed an electrical nature which groped after hidden elements of discomfort and pleasure, and repelled the foreign or appropriated her own whenever she found either. She could enter a room full of strangers and select those whom she would like and who would like her before speaking to any of them.

In this instance she knew that there was a disturbing element present. She wondered what it was. She set herself quietly to observe and to wrest the true cause from some one unaware.

Alice was quiet and subdued — no longer the Alice of West Point. The judge too had lost some of the assured charm of manner which comes from a sensitive nature feeling itself constantly approved of. Kate smiled to realize that even she felt in a measure quieted, for Mrs. Copeland had a dignified way of making her guests feel the honor of being beneath her distinguished roof.

Miss Vandevoort, who loved children, suddenly spied Elsie, lean, sallow, and unlovely, and moved by pity for so forlorn a specimen of petted childhood, turned and greeted her kindly. But to her unspeakable dismay Elsie immediately burst into tears and thrust herself behind her mother.

"Oh, Miss Vandevoort, I neglected to tell you," said Mrs. Copeland, "that we never speak suddenly to Elsie like that. My child is very timid, and I have been three days persuading her to come into the drawing-room at all to-night. She suffers so from hysteria. We approach her very cautiously."

The corners of Kate's mouth twitched. When she found it was hysteria, and not that the child had cut her hand off or burst a blood-vessel, it was with difficulty that Kate kept herself from jumping at Elsie and giving her something to cry for.

"How sadly the child is afflicted," sighed Mrs. Overshine.

Kate suddenly remembered that everybody in Stockbridge had a chronic ailment, and this incident revealed in a flash how they were acquired. Realizing a neglected duty, she said, with well simulated sympathy, "Do tell me, dear Mrs. Copeland, how is your poor head?"

"It is very bad, thank you, Miss Vandevoort. Some days I am truly wretched with it. Oh, no one knows my sufferings."

"What a pity! And you look so well, too. No one would believe you were such a martyr if he did not hear the statement from your own lips. And the judge, is his—his dyspepsia better?"

"Well, not very much. He spent a sleepless night, and, as you see, looks pale this evening."

"And Gifford, is he quite well?"

"No, Gifford cut his wrist with a penknife yesterday, and I persuaded him to have the doctor see it. He said if it had been two inches higher it might have been serious."

"How fortunate those two inches are! And George, has he arrived?"

"No, he is still in New York, and I am afraid

he is ill. I wrote him a ten-page letter, filled with advice about his health, and telling him all the primary symptoms of several diseases that I hear are prevailing there, and pleading with him as only a mother can, to sit down and think if he felt any of them, and if so, to telegraph which and to see a doctor at once. But I have had no reply."

"How anxious you must be," said Kate, earnestly. "And Alice, here; it seems to me that she looks too quiet and sad to be quite well."

"Yes, Alice practises too much. She has a weak back, I think."

"Mamma, I am perfectly well," said Alice.

"I know you think so, dear, but your eyes look heavy. Oh, Alice is far from well. We are none of us strong."

"Indeed, Mrs. Copeland, I can see that you are not. If asked my opinion, I should be obliged to admit that you enjoyed poor health."

Alice regarded Kate gravely. She never countenanced a word either in fun or in earnest which held her mother up to ridicule. But Miss Vandevoort apparently saw nothing amusing in what she had said, and Mrs. Copeland was Scotch.

Kate immediately repented her impertinent little speech, which nobody except Colonel Overshine had recognized. She turned away from the spectacle of his red face, and said to the judge:

"It was beautiful of you, Judge Copeland, to make such a noble gift to Stockbridge as that fine Public Library. Mollie and I have been all over it to-day, and although I tried with all the ingenuity at my command, I could find not the slightest flaw in it."

"And would you have been so happy to find it imperfect, Miss Vandevoort?" said Mrs. Copeland, in a colorless voice, which sent little shivers of aversion shuddering all the way to Kate's finger-tips.

Judge Copeland smiled at her benignantly, and Mrs. Overshine hastened to say:

"Kate was so enthusiastic over it that I could hardly drag her away. She always acts as if books were human and understood her when she tells each one why she loves it. We had the children with us, and that very thing showed the difference between them. Frances clung to Kate's hand, shrieking in delight at Kate's fantastic speeches to her pet books, speeches which Frances did not entirely comprehend, but she caught at the meaning sufficiently to grasp the fun of the situation. But Peggy, together with two or three old ladies standing near—Mrs. Troutman and Mrs. Frazer, Chris—looked at her as if they thought her simply a harmless lunatic."

"Oh, is Mrs. Frazer well enough to be out?" said Mrs. Copeland. "I heard that this new treatment was helping her. She has had nervous prostration for fourteen years, and her mother died of heart disease. There is consumption in the family, too. It is a marvel to me that she is alive to-day. I think she shows a wonderful vitality."

"Yes, she was out to-day, and looking quite well for her," answered Mrs. Overshine.

"I notice that she always gets well enough to be out when there is anything going on," observed Colonel Overshine, with a twinkle in his eye. "She hadn't seen the new Library, so she partially recovered again."

Mrs. Overshine cleared her throat at him as a warning.

"Her wonderful vitality evidences itself in quite marvellous partial recoveries, Kate," he continued, disregarding his wife's signals of distress, which nevertheless he saw perfectly.

Kate raised her lace handkerchief to her lips, and felt, rather than saw, the sudden stiffening of the backbone of her hostess.

Mrs. Overshine shook her head imploringly at her husband.

"She will go to bed again to-morrow," pursued Colonel Overshine, ruthlessly, "until another small excitement occurs. Then she will be 'able to be out' once more."

"She is perfectly honest in her illness, Colonel

Overshine," said Mrs. Copeland, coldly. "There is a great deal of suffering in Stockbridge. I wanted the judge to build a hospital instead of a library, but he had his own way about it, as usual."

"Oh, my dear wife, there was no controversy about it. Pray assure our friends of that."

"No, because I gave up my way at once. I always do."

"Why, I thought you were quite pleased with the idea of the library," said the judge, with a note of anxiety in his voice.

It seems as if some men never *would* see the justice of the way a woman who has been affronted by somebody else takes it out on her husband, or whoever happens to be handy.

"You know perfectly well that I should have preferred a hospital."

"I suppose, dear Mrs. Copeland," put in Colonel Overshine, repenting too late for the turn he had given the conversation, "that the judge thought Stockbridge was more in need of encouragement along the line of the library. In this town sickness reaches perfection through its own impetus."

Mrs. Copeland drew back her chin in silent displeasure. Mrs. Overshine mentally washed her hands of her husband, who then looked at his ally, Kate, for the approval which the honest gentleman really expected to follow this well-meant jocularity.

8

But Kate, in response to a telegram from Mollie, had turned her back on him. They meant to make him feel his disgrace.

When dinner was announced, Elsie refused to move, so after politely hanging back and wondering what was going to happen next, all except Mrs. Copeland proceeded to the dining-room, where presently Mrs. Copeland appeared, with Elsie hiding her face in her mother's skirts and half walking on her train.

"If you don't look at her or notice her," whispered Mrs. Copeland, "perhaps she will be all right."

Accordingly they began an animated discussion about nothing at all, while Mrs. Copeland coaxed Elsie, who still hid her face and occasionally wept. Judge Copeland watched the contest thoughtfully, but said nothing. Alice's face flushed uncomfortably, but she never thought of interfering. Colonel and Mrs. Overshine were used to it, but Kate's fingers fairly twitched to jerk Elsie into her chair in short order, and have done with such nonsense. How civilization steps in in such a crisis! Kate merely sighed, and murmured, "Poor child!"

Before the soup was removed, however, Elsie consented to get into her chair, provided it were changed from her mother's left to her right. Colonel Overshine accordingly offered to move, and Elsie sat in the vacated chair with her hair pulled over her eyes.

Frank Overshine, with his kind, wide smile and genuine simplicity, was told off to Alice, who made spasmodic efforts to entertain him while she tried to listen to every word that Kate uttered.

The dinner was exquisitely appointed and served, but Elsie cried twice, and finally Mrs. Copeland took her from the table.

"The dear child," she murmured, as she returned.

Everybody gurgled something in reply, and then Mrs. Overshine said,

"I hear that George and his friend, Mr. Counselman, will soon be here."

"George will come next week, but as we expect another guest, Mr. Counselman is not coming."

"Ah, ha," thought Miss Vandervoort. "The other guest means, I think, my friend Senator Cobb. Poor Alice. How can they? How can they?"

"Oh, I am so sorry Gordon Counselman isn't coming," she said. "He is such a lovely fellow, and so clever. Colonel Sheldon told me that he had done more towards the suppression of hazing at West Point than any other cadet who ever entered there. He is such a strong character that he could not fail of influencing any one with whom he came in contact. He is a great friend of George's, Mrs.

Copeland. I am glad your son had the good taste to like him."

"Kate, was he the one I overheard you telling Mollie about—the one who was in the toils of poor Jim Verry's gay widow?" asked Col. Overshine.

"Oh, no indeed. That was Mr. Pratt. Mrs. Verry paid attention to Gordon last year—she is the boldest thing—but Gordon confided to me, in his frank, boyish way, which gets such a hold on my heartstrings, that he really thought Mrs. Verry was hardly as modest and ladylike as he liked to see women. I could scarcely keep my face straight, for she had toned herself down many shades in order to captivate Gordon's well-known taste. I wonder what the boy would have said of her if he could see her with her usual racing colors on."

"By Jove, I'd like to have been at West Point with you, Kate. You see so much."

"Well, I don't go to sleep, Chris, if you mean that. I keep my eyes open. But, dear me, there is so much to see."

"What is Mrs. Verry doing now?" asked Colonel Overshine.

"Why, she spends most of her time hating me, because, for some unaccountable reason, she thinks I interfere with her Senator Cobb."

"*Her* Senator Cobb!" repeated Mrs. Copeland, regarding Kate gravely, then looking pointedly at the judge and then at Alice, as if to say " How do you explain that?"

"Yes, indeed," answered Kate, with what Alice recognized as her innocent look. "Hers, dear Mrs. Copeland. Not mine, nor yours, nor anybody's except Mrs. Verry's—so she thinks. I don't know why she should be jealous of *me*. To be sure, he sent me flowers once—Alice, you remember—but, if she only knew it, she need not dread me."

"Why, what's the matter with him? He must be queer if you won't have anything to do with him."

"Now, Cousin Mollie, isn't he unkind to me? Why, Chris, all that's the matter with him only adds to his dignity. It is his age. Senator Cobb is mediæval, and I don't go in for the antique."

"Gray hairs are honorable, Miss Vandevoort," said Mrs. Copeland, who labored under the delusion that it was proper to reprove a guest under her roof for anything she saw amiss in her.

Like many other good women, with excellent Stockbridge intentions and high ideals in tatting, Mrs. Copeland was her brother's keeper to such a rigorous extent that her spiritual brother often longed to go from her presence straight to the broad way which leadeth to destruction, just for a relish. Not only did she look after her son and her daughter and her man servant and her maid servant and her ox and her ass, but she also found time to attend to the moral well-being of every other ox and ass in all Stockbridge.

"Yes, but, dear Mrs. Copeland," said Kate, sweetly, "his are not gray. If they were, and there were more of them, they might inspire your respect. But his hair is so thin, and he wears it long, so that a strong draught lifts it now and then and exhibits its thinness cruelly. He is lean, too, and he wears side-whiskers (I might forgive the first, but not the second), and they are not all the same length or the same color, so that he reminds you of a piece of moth-eaten fur. He is a pale, straw-colored man all through. If he were a horse, you would call him a clay-bank.

"And furthermore, dear Mrs. Copeland, if you ever happen to meet him, for my sake, notice his peculiar smile; and I know why it is so. He has the expansive smile of a man when he first wears false teeth after having had much trouble with his old ones. He used to have to hold his upper lip down when he laughed, but it is such a relief to him to feel now that he can smile, grin, even roar, if he chooses, that in an excess of ease and relief he relaxes his vigilance to the extent of showing where his teeth join, and sometimes, if the jest is an excellent one, even giving a good idea of the plate itself. Of course there is no harm in this," added Miss Vandevoort, genially, looking around to include everybody, "only it is a little trying on the person opposite. If he were wretchedly poor, he would be a pathetic figure, and you would want to send him a red flannel nightcap for his poor old head, and a warm wadded dressing-gown for his poor thin legs. As a grandfather in a chimney-corner he would be a great success. But as it is, he is so rich that he is simply nauseating, aud so abundantly satisfied with himself and so complacent that his smiles are an irritation and his whiskers an insult."

Alice's radiant face was a reward which even the grim expression on Mrs. Copeland's failed to spoil. Kate was sure, from the uneasy manner in which the judge watched his wife and Alice, during her wicked speech, that affairs had come to a crisis with Senator Cobb, and that poor Gordon's chances looked dubious indeed.

When she got home that night she shook her fist at herself in the glass.

"I hate you, Kate Vandevoort, when you ridicule a man's physical imperfections. You think yourself so clever. Why couldn't you have thought up a better way to help that poor girl than so to degrade yourself in your own sight. Oh, poor Kate! You do try so hard to be good, but it is such desperately weary work, and there is nothing, absolutely nothing, in all this beautiful world for you to look forward to, except to be of use to those who are weaker than you. No love, no home, no fireside of your own. Just always to be an on-looker at the feast of others; to feel the warmth of others' fires and to go shivering yourself. Oh, the pity of it! The horrible pity of life! Can I see Alice wreck hers as mine has been wrecked? See her eat her heart out in the utter hopelessness of her just meed of joy? No, no"—her voice sank to a whisper—"no matter how hard it is, I must go on with it—as *he* would have had me."

IX

THE CHILD PROBLEM

Dull people, or those who have only stupid children, may well be excused for declaring that the bewildering precocity of the John Vandevoort children was unnatural and wellnigh impossible. Kate herself, although an eye and ear witness of it, often went away from them with an uncanny sense of the supernatural. Their sense of humor was so adult, their cynicism so unsteadying. It can only be accounted for in the facts that they had been parties from their babyhood to the marital unhappiness of their father and mother, and the constant companions of clever but unwise grown people, who openly discussed social problems before them in a manner which could not fail of impressing the dullest intellects. Falling as it did upon snapping little brains, alert to hear and learn, it turned the Vandevoort children into amateur philosophers, whose sayings were a real terror to those who held their precious little souls dear.

That they adored their aunt Kate it is needless to say. She was just picturesque enough to appeal to their quick imaginations, and in return she made wild efforts to understand them. She succeeded to the extent that they confided in her in preference to their mother, and often said if Aunt Kate could only have been their mother, their parents would have been perfect.

The unhappy example of the supreme selfishness of their mother, whose beauty they admired, but for whom they had very little affection, drove Kate to seek out every possible opportunity to let them, in the same manner, share the lovelier traits of humanity. Otherwise she dared not face their future. The poor little things, with all that culture and wealth and travel could give, had been given no chance to learn the weightier matters of the law, justice, mercy, and truth.

Colonel Overshine was their obedient slave from the moment they entered his house. He vowed that Frances was more entertaining than all the grown-up people in Stockbridge put together, and that round-eyed Peggy could wheedle the nose off his face, if she set her mind to do it. Kate arranged their studies for them. They already chattered in French and German as fluently as she herself, so she gave them drawing and music, on condition that they should learn spelling and arithmetic.

Their manners in public would have put Beau Brummell to the blush, but in private Frances was a little demon, and Peggy would fight as quietly but as long as a bull-dog. Frances flew into a passion a dozen times a day, but was ready to kiss and apologize in two minutes. Peggy would stand almost anything, but when once her anger against her sister began to burn with a slow white heat, she had to be peeled off of Frances like a plaster. She stuck to her in absolute silence, no matter what her own injuries, with never a sound except Frances's yells and screams. Only Kate could silence them. They obeyed her because they adored yet feared her. They walked over their father's authority because they knew that they could.

They had been in Stockbridge about two months when Miss Vandevoort came down from New York to pay this promised visit to Cousin Mollie Overshine. She had been down several times during July, stopping over for a day in flitting from mountains to sea-shore; but this time her stay was to be longer, and the children cast themselves upon her in rapturous delight.

Kate sympathized with Frances the most, because everybody preferred stupid little Peggy's sweetness to her older sister's too clever intelligence.

Nobody could take any comfort with as sharp a child as Frances, and people made no secret of their preference for the soothing companionship of her fat little sister. Most people prefer a pincushion to an emery—for daily use.

One morning as Kate came out of the house with a telegram in her hand, she found Frances on the veranda with her spelling-book.

"What are you doing, lamb?"

"Learning to spell, Aunt Kate, so that I can write letters to you that you won't be ashamed of."

"How nice that will be, and how proud I shall be of them. But do you want to stop now and give a great deal of pleasure to somebody?"

"Oh, I should like to well enough, if I were not doing something more important."

"Is there anything more important than deliberately to put a pleasure into somebody's life?"

"Oh, I think so. It is more important to speak French. It is more important to play on the piano. It is more important to sing well, so that when I enter society I can be as much admired and have as many lovers as you have."

"Who told you anything about my lovers?" asked Kate, sternly.

"Mamma. She often talked to us about them. She said you were an awful fool not to marry Sir James Whitehall. She said she thought your success had turned your head, because you kept refusing such fine offers, and that you would pick up a crooked stick after all. I asked her what a crooked stick meant, and she said papa was one. I told her I hoped you would marry a crooked stick then, and she slapped me."

"Good heavens!" said Kate, sitting down in a big wicker rocking-chair and drawing Frances into her lap, regardless of her fresh muslin dress that the child crushed.

"I am afraid I'll spoil your dress if I lean my head against your shoulder," said Frances.

"Never mind if you do. I like the feel of your little head, just to make sure that you *are* a little child, and not a misshapen, grown-up, warped soul with a dwarf's body. Poor little dear! You've never had half a chance. I ought not to be angry with you, my lamb; but it nearly kills me to hear you talk in that manner."

"Oh, Auntie Kate, don't look that way! I won't speak all day. I'll do anything for you, if you will just tell me. *I* didn't know I was saying anything to make you sorry. Perhaps you are sorry because Mamma slapped me? Pooh! that wasn't anything. She slapped us whenever anything went wrong, whether we did it or not. But the time she slapped and shook us till our heads most fell off—she's awful strong—was when she used to get hysterics and scream, and Peggy and I would screech and yell just like her, to see who could yell the loudest.

My, but she gave it to us then! Hortense pretended to help her, but she got us away from her and locked us in the nursery till Mamma cooled down. Then she let us out, and we went to drive in the victoria, and lots of people looked at us and said, 'What lovely children!' just as if they wished theirs were like us. I felt like saying, 'Well, you wouldn't, if you knew the inside of us.'"

Kate only went on rocking her in silence. For once she had nothing to say.

"I wish you were my mother," said Frances, suddenly. "Lieber Katechen! You would make an awfully nice mother. You know how to treat children. Mamma doesn't. Mamma ought to have stayed a bachelor. What are you laughing at? Isn't that the right word? I told that to Cousin Chris, and he laughed so, he most shook me off his lap. Cousin Mollie said I meant 'spinster,' but Cousin Chris said, 'No, leave it bachelor. That word describes Emily Vandevoort to a T.' Mamma does not approve of marriage for anybody. When she meets a young lady in society, she takes her hand, like this, and she says, '*Miss* Gilbert, allow me to congratulate you that it is not as *Mrs.* Somebody that I must address you.'"

"Good heavens!" cried Kate, setting Frances up in her lap and holding her two arms down tightly, "what an awful thing to hear the cynicism of the world brought home by such baby lips as yours! Stop thinking about such things. Come, don't you want to go with me to see Miss Alice Copeland? I have a telegram in my hand which will make her eyes shine so that you could see them in the dark."

"Like a cat under the bed," said Frances, who was nothing if not a believer in applied science.

"Well, that is hardly as poetical as to liken them to stars in heaven, but it does very well, and certainly no one could misunderstand you."

Frances laughed shrilly.

"You are making fun," she declared. "I love to hear people make fun. Nobody ever does it at our house any more. But whenever I go out, I always laugh every chance I get."

She darted away to get ready, and came back swinging her hat by one of the ribbons.

"Don't make me put it on," she begged as they started. "I always have to be so prim when I walk in New York with Hortense, with her eternal 'Prenez-garde, ma chère,' and her always clawing our skirts down and our hair back. That's why I just *love* Stockbridge. It is so still, and the trees rustle so, and the grass is so soft and green, and I haven't seen a single sign 'Keep off the grass' since we have been here. In India once a man asked Papa what our national motto was, and he said the only national motto that we enforced was 'Keep off the grass,' and everybody laughed except the Englishman who asked him. He believed it, Papa said."

"Your father also told a man in London that our national dish was pie."

"Pie? And he believed it, didn't he? That's what Papa said is the funny part."

"Yes, he believed it."

"What makes people fool Englishmen so?"

"Oh, because they never know anything about America. It's so lovely to see what impossible statements they will believe."

"Why don't they know about America?"

"Because they don't want to. I suppose they like to be provincial."

"Provincial? What's provincial?"

"Let me see. Why, provincial means liking your own little hole in the world so much that you never stick your head outside of it to see if there is anything else."

"Don't English people know about anything but England?"

"Two or three of them do."

"Well, we know about them."

"Oh yes; that's fashionable."

"But isn't it fashionable for them to know about us?"

"No, it is fashionable for them not to know about us."

"Is that what makes Englishmen so funny?"

"Yes," said Kate, laughing. "That is exactly what makes Englishmen so funny."

"Just look at this lovely grass," sighed the child, running her eyes hungrily over the meadows and lawns.

"If you love grass so much, you should see the prairies out West," said Kate.

"Out West?" repeated Frances. "I don't think I should care to go out West. Mamma says that New York is all of America that I need to see."

"Take care, little Miss Provincial! Won't you stick your head out of your little hole and take a look at the beautiful world beyond? Or do you want to be as funny as an Englishman?"

"Can you be provincial in America?" asked Frances, opening her eyes.

"Certainly. The worst kind of provincialism is the American, because that is all put on, and the English is real. *They* were born that way."

"Oh, I hate anybody who 'puts on.'"

"Then don't turn up that nose of yours at America, because you haven't seen any of it yet."

"Stockbridge is nice," said Frances. "I like it because I can play with the coachman's children. Mamma never lets me in New York. But I don't see why. Sometimes I want to play with them worse than anything else in the world. My geography says that people don't all belong to the same race. The Chinese are Mongolians, and we are Caucasians. Now, the coachman's children belong to the barn race, and I belong to the house race. That's all the difference. And sometimes I think the barn race has the best time."

Kate was immensely amused, and yet a little terrified. She found herself telling the child things as she would to a grown person. It was impossible not to respect such intelligence, no matter how childish the body. But then Kate Vandevoort was so queer. She actually respected childhood, and saw wonderful possibilities of individualism in little souls which other people, older and wiser than she, were sorting into batches and labelling alike. She wondered what kind of a woman Frances would make. Either a very bad one or a very good one. By her daily life she would either teach the way upward or set a fearful example of what to avoid. But, at any rate, interesting — interesting! And that is half the battle. Interesting to old and young, to high and low alike. Even as a child, Kate felt that Frances had the gift of feeling the heart of humanity.

"There is where Miss Copeland lives," said Kate.

"Is it? That great house on the terrace, with white pillars like the Parthenon?"

Kate looked down at her, seized with a physical weakness. She doubted if she herself should have associated Corinthian columns with anything more elevated than the White House.

"What do you remember about the Parthenon, you baby?"

"Why, didn't I ever tell you? Mamma and Papa had an awful quarrel there. Papa wanted to go to see it again by moonlight, but she wouldn't. She said once was enough, and she called him an awful fool for wanting to go. So he came into our room with his lips set together like this, and had Hortense take me up and dress me; and he carried me there and told me to look at it and remember it. And I did. And it was the most beautiful thing I ever saw in all my life, but so lonesome. And he kissed me most a hundred times when I said so, and he said I belonged to him. But he left a tear on my cheek, and it scared me so I've never forgotten it."

She paused at the gate.

"There are Peggy and Hortense!" she declared. "Don't call them over. Leave them, and let's go in alone."

"Come, come, none of that, Miss Piggy Selfishness. Suppose you go home and leave me to go in alone. Haven't we come to be generous with Miss Copeland about the telegram?"

"Yes, but it's so much easier to be generous with other people than with your sister."

"Then all the more credit to you when you share with Peggy. It is only people like you and me, who would much rather be bad, who deserve any credit for being good."

"You are good naturally, lieber Kätchen."

"Not a bit of it. There are times when I want to tear things wide open, and scream, and break things, just the way you do."

"But you *never do it*," said Frances, aghast at the picture.

"Certainly not. I won't allow myself to. I always think how silly it must look to good people who never lose their temper."

Frances colored.

"And to the angels," she said, softly.

Kate squeezed her hand with sudden feeling.

"Shall we be bad now, and not let Peggy come, or shall we be good?"

"Will you do just as I say?" asked Frances, curiously.

"Yes; but remember, if you lead me into temptation, it will be a double sin for you."

"But if I say to send Peggy back home, will you do it, and take me in alone?" she insisted.

"Yes."

"Then call Peggy. Or, no, let me call her. Allons, Peggy! Hortense! Venez ici. Venez avec nous. Nous allons faire une visite à Mademoiselle Copeland. Voudriez-vous venir?"

"Oh, ja, ja!" cried Peggy, who was so Dutch, with her fat legs and Gretchen braids, that she spoke her German from preference.

"Parlez français, mademoiselle," said Hortense, angrily, with a sharp pull at the child's hand.

"Hortense," said Miss Vandevoort, quietly.

"Je vous demande pardon, mademoiselle."

"Parlez avec plus de douceur, je vous prie. Laissez les enfants parler allemand quand ils veulent."

"Je vous demande pardon, mademoiselle, mais je déteste l'allemand."

"Oui, je le sais, mais je le veux."

"C'est assez, mademoiselle," said Hortense, with a smile.

Servants always adored Kate, and Hortense had been such a faithful creature and so discreet through all the family trouble that Kate was particularly fond of her. Her chief fault was that she waged a perpetual war with the German governess.

When Frances was good, she was very, very good, and also, like the little girl with the immortal curl in the middle of her immortal forehead, "when she was bad, she was horrid." However, it was almost worth a tantrum to put her into the celestial state of mind which always followed an outburst, and to which she now had attained through her forbearance towards Peggy, whose fat legs were toiling up the steps of the terrace just ahead of her. Peggy reached the top with scarlet cheeks and the breath almost pumped from her short body. But the little, thin, nervous face of Frances was ethereally beautiful. Her coal-black curls, loose almost to straightness, hung around her pale cheeks like a frame, and her great velvet eyes never left Kate's face, as she humbly clung to her hand, like a tamed spirit of the air.

Never was there anything prettier or more ladylike than the way in which she greeted Mrs. Copeland, whom they found upon the terrace, going up to her to be presented with the quiet self-possession of a woman of the world. She looked with amazement upon Elsie, who refused to look up or speak to Miss Vandevoort, and who, when she lifted her head from her mother's lap, only stared at Peggy and Frances in shy, stubborn silence.

Frances instinctively held aloof from Mrs. Copeland, recognizing the coldness in her face, although much more interested in her than Elsie. But, as usual, Peggy, the little round diplomat, who would not have given a crumb where Frances would have given her last crust or the whole loaf, engagingly climbed upon Mrs. Copeland's black satin knee, and artfully coiled herself in the iron receptacle which served that austere woman for a heart.

Mrs. Copeland was graciously pleased to invite the children to lunch with Elsie. Peggy accepted joyfully, scrambling down from Mrs. Copeland's lap and trotting up to the house without a backward glance. Frances, who much preferred the society of grown people, hung back until Kate sent her after the rest.

Kate afterwards remembered the beautiful expression of her face, and she knew what a genius for irritation Mrs. Copeland must possess, in order to stir up the storm in which that unhappy luncheon or dinner ended.

X

ON THE BOAT-HOUSE STEPS

WHEN Mrs. Copeland drew from her pocket her fancy work, and settled back in the rustic seat where they had found her, Alice, in obedience to a gesture from Kate, proposed that they should go down to the boat-house.

"What is the matter with you, Alice?" said Kate, when they were alone.

"Oh, nothing. What makes you ask?"

"Oh, nothing."

Kate laughed roguishly.

"Aren't you going to tell me?"

"There's nothing to tell."

"When is Senator Cobb coming to propose to you?"

"How did you know he was going to?" asked Alice, startled.

"I didn't. I only wanted to know. Are you going to accept him?"

"I don't know. They—"

"You don't know! They—!" cried Kate, with a shake of Alice's shoulder that made her bite her tongue. "How dare you hint at such a thing? Do you mean to tell me that you love that awful old man?"

"No, no," cried Alice, covering her face with her hands.

"Then has that precious mother of yours urged you into it?"

"Urged? Urged? I never hear anything else. She is going to *make* me! I don't dare to refuse."

"You little coward!"

"Yes, but you don't know my mother. You don't know her. You don't know her."

Alice evidently could not gain her own consent to say more.

"What does your father say?"

"He says for me to do as I will. He never even said that much before when anything went against mother's wishes. He always wants me to do as she says."

"Wouldn't your father befriend you if you refused in this case?"

"I don't know. He would stand between us, I think, if I could only tell him."

"Why don't you tell him?"

"Oh, I couldn't. It seems so — so indelicate."

"Alice Copeland, I *hope* there is nobody else in the world exactly like you."

"Why, *I* think that is a sign of refinement," said Alice, primly.

"I know you do, my dear. And if you don't beware, you will approve of your own refinement to such an extent that you will turn out an unconscionable little prig. You don't seem to mind dealing me a rap into the bargain, but I do not care particularly, for it is only the result of Stockbridge and Presbyterianism and the pharisaic atmosphere you breathe. Your bad manners do not come from an unkind heart. Consequently you only lack tact. But for the sake of your friend myself, I pray Heaven you may acquire that soon."

"I have hurt your feelings," said Alice, remorsefully.

"Yes, you have hurt my feelings, because I am only a publican and a sinner, and because I live in a wicked city where publicans are liked and approved of, and where we seldom get a rap over the nose such as you just dealt to me."

"Oh, I am so sorry."

"I don't lay it up against you, because I hardly see how you could be anything else with the exam — ahem! — with such surroundings. Good heavens, Alice! You ought to go around the world, and get a point of view."

Alice looked up, startled by Miss Vandevoort's vehemence. "A point of view?" she repeated, doubtfully.

"Yes, yes; a point of view! Is anything more maddening than to go ambling peacefully along in life, smiling at the world and harming nobody, and suddenly to dash your head against the stone wall of provincial virtue, and lie on your back for a while, seeing red and green stars? I really think there is an element of viciousness in the virtue of a small town which is worse than loose-slippered liberality. I think narrowness, whenever and wherever you meet it, is the most irritating of all the vices. Of course, I am a woman, and I can only talk and rage about these things in a perfectly ladylike and refined way; but they make me desperate."

"Do *I* make you feel like that?" asked Alice.

"Oh, no, not quite yet," said Miss Vandevoort, rumpling her hair with whimsical fretfulness. "But I am afraid of what you are going to be. You have set your feet on the slippery downward path of Perfection, and I only wish you could see how stupidly conceited you appear to a pagan outsider, because you believe so absolutely that you are right and that I am wrong. Now I don't agree with you. I am wrong enough, Heaven knows, only you are more wrong than I. It is but a question of degree. You can't see it, and you are not believing me right now, because you are looking at me from the point of view of Stockbridge, Potts County, Pennsylvania. You are a different creature here from the girl I knew at West Point. Do you remember the night of the hop?"

Alice turned her head away and made no reply at first. They were sitting at the foot of the terrace, on the steps leading up from the boat-house. The summer had been very hot and dry so far, and the Delaware was sinking rapidly. Kate sat watching the shadows on the river, and wondering how to broach the subject of the telegram, when she was startled by Alice's voice, with a little ring of hardness in it, saying,

"After all, why not — m - marry him? I don't want to live in Stockbridge forever and be narrow and provincial."

"Well, dear me, is there no one else except Senator Cobb? What has become of all the other men in the world since we have been sitting here? Has a pestilence swept them from the face of the earth?"

"There is no one else who cares for me," said Alice, bitterly.

"How do you know?"

"Mother says so."

"Um. Does she?"

"Yes, she does. And I know that it is true."

"*Do* you! You are very wise."

If Kate expected to sting Alice by her tone into either question or explanation, she was disappointed, for Kate was finally obliged to say, "How about Gordon Counselman?"

Alice turned and faced her vehemently. "There is nothing about him!" she declared.

"How do you know? Don't you, in your secret heart, believe that he loves you?"

Kate was not sure that Alice would not plunge headlong into the river at the open mention of such an indelicate fact. But to her surprise she found that Alice, like most reticent persons, occasionally fairly revelled in the opening up of a closed subject.

"No, I don't."

"Why?"

"Why? Because I have not had a letter from him for a month. Why did he stop writing? Why did he promise to come home with George and then suddenly withdraw his acceptance without any reason or any explanation?"

"Why?" repeated Kate, excitedly. "Because your mother wrote to him and withdrew her son's invitation in such a way that Gordon could not explain even to George, and there is a coolness between them now, because George is too proud to ask why, and Gordon too much of a gentleman to 'show a fellow's mother up to him in an unfavorable light.'

And most of all, because Mrs. Copeland gave Gordon to understand that you were engaged to Senator Cobb. *That* is why Gordon does not write. Your mother intimated that she wrote in your behalf to break the news to him."

Alice reached out for Kate's hand to steady herself.

"My mother did that? My *mother?*"

She kept repeating it, as if she could not take it in, and she looked so dazed that Kate hurriedly put the telegram into her hand.

"Read that. Mollie has invited him to our house, and he is coming to-morrow. To-morrow, do you hear?"

Alice read the telegram twice, and laughed hysterically.

"And Senator Cobb is coming to-night and I shall be engaged by to-morrow. Don't you see that I can't help myself? Don't you know that my mother has succeeded in everything she ever undertook in her life? Don't you know that she will marry me to the senator if it kills me? I didn't know before how determined she was. But if she has done all this, I might as well give up at once."

"Poor Gordon," said Kate, softly.

Alice clutched her hand.

"Do you think he cares?"

"I know that he cares. I only wish you had been noble enough to have faith in him—such faith as he would have had in you."

Alice shook her head. "I am not noble. I have no faith."

"You have no courage, and no hope, either," said Kate, in a vexed tone.

Alice looked up at her humbly.

"I know—I know," said Kate, hastily. "Perhaps I shouldn't have, either, in your place. But are you going to give up like that? Aren't you going to nerve yourself?"

"What is the use? Don't you know that I am bound hand and foot? Have *you* ever contended with my mother? Do you know how futile it is?"

"It wouldn't be for me!" cried Kate, wickedly. "I'd just *love* to pit my will against hers!"

"Yours!" said Alice. "Why, her will would grind yours to powder. Yours makes more noise, but hers is as quiet and deadly as—as the grave. I should as soon think of contending with Death."

"Well, I believe that there is such a thing as contesting the field with Death," began Kate, boldly. Then she covered her face with her hands, and a groan burst from her lips. "Oh, God, forgive me for saying that!" she murmured. "Once I did contest the field with Death, and Death won."

"Oh, dear Miss Vandevoort," cried Alice, putting her arms around Kate, and forgetting herself in a moment, as she always did in the face of another's trouble.

Kate sat up suddenly and took both of Alice's hands in hers, and looked into her eyes with a look which went clear through the world's ways, down, down into the girl's soul.

"Once—how long ago it seems, measured by everything but years!—I stood just where you are standing now, with the privilege of choosing my life's happiness or its misery. It was even more in my power to choose freely than it is in yours. Alice, if I did not love you I could not tell you this. You don't know why I love you, do you? It is because you remind me of myself. Once I was as single-hearted as you. My environments were not like yours, but they fettered me quite as much, and in the writhing of my spirit to free myself they turned me into the complex creature I am to-day, with so much of good and ill warring in my soul that sometimes it frightens me even now, coolheaded as I love to believe myself. Alice, I was meant to be a true woman. I feel it, but I couldn't help being influenced, I couldn't help being dragged down. I couldn't keep my ideals high and clean when every passer-by dashed them down. So I lowered them inch by inch myself, until they were on a level with my eyes and I no longer had to look up to see them. Then they were not ideals any more. They were my familiars. But I could not bear their reproachful faces. So I wrapped them in sophistry and put them further away. I knew they were within reach. I did not wish to destroy them, but they were only dim, shadowy shapes, and I tried to forget them, for it hurt me to think of them.

"I was not happy even then, but I filled every hour so full that I could not think. I was reckless in those days, afraid to stop and see where I was. Everybody envied me. I was supposed to be perfectly happy. I said I was. I tried to believe it. But I never succeeded. In my heart I hated the ways of society, and loathed myself for conforming to them.

"Then I met for the second time a man I once had known and forgotten. From the moment I knew him I felt how I must appear to him—how shallow, heartless, worldly. He made me see myself, and oh, how I suffered! He was so different from the other men I knew, and I was so proud because he seemed attracted to me. He was a cadet at West Point, and I had gone up there with my father and mother to spend the summer.

"Max never cared for other girls, and I was flattered that I had won the attentions of the most difficult man at West Point. But it was only an outward victory, for although he was always with me, yet he held himself, his real self, aloof from me. I felt that it was because he did not approve of me, perhaps because he could not respect me. Love makes a women either proud or humble, Alice. It humbled me, and this new thought stung me to the quick. I resolved to make myself different—to be so good that he would love me. I wanted him to love me. And although I spent the days and nights in anxiety, I look back on that summer as the happiest of my life, for no matter how hard the struggle, there is nothing so sweet as to try of your own accord to make yourself better for the one you love, when it is all your own secret. I should hate a man who *wanted* me to be better!

"Most unfortunately for us, Max was poor and I was rich. I really think that I myself never should have thought of this. But my father"—and Kate's face flushed at the recollection of it—"my father said that a gentleman should never feel the lack of money. Absurd as it sounds to me now, knowing as I do that according to that theory there are very few gentleman in the world, nevertheless when one is younger one feels such things much more keenly. I was sensitive and foolish and young—three most unfortunate things according to my way of thinking now—and I felt on raw nerves every one of the stings which his keen sarcastic wit was capable of making at Max's expense.

"This is not a very noble love story I am telling you, is it Alice? Make excuses for me, if you can. Not that I excuse myself, but I have suffered enough since to wipe out every sin I ever committed with drops of my heart's blood.

"Max felt the difference in our positions even more than my father did, although I did not know it, and I was not noble enough, when I began to love him, to ascribe any virtues to him which I had not seen in other men. I loved him simply because I could not help myself. I was walking by sight and not by faith, and just at that time my sight was not very lofty. I had a contempt for most men. Such hosts of them had made love to me. Some were too stupid to conceal that my fortune would be no drawback. Some were too eager, simply because I had pleased their eye, to deceive even a *young* girl as to their real selves. Some were too business-like to satisfy the sentimental side of my nature. Some were too young for me not to know that I overtopped them mentally; some too old ever to learn anything new; but most of them too gross not to repel as sensitive a creature as I, and I loathed them all for daring to call themselves in love with me. I suppose they thought they were. I suppose they believed in themselves. But, to my mind, they never knew the meaning of the word. And so, in spite of lofty ideals, and wanting to believe in men, the very men themselves dragged their sex down for me, and lowered my standard of men, and drove me further and further toward the material side of humanity.

"So when I would have believed in Max, my worldly wisdom stepped in and held me back, and made me misjudge him. Then when still he held off from me in words, while letting me read in every other way, as a man will, even when he doesn't mean to, that he loved me, my ease-loving, pleasure-choosing nature revolted against the cruelty and hardship of loving a man with all my heart who didn't or wouldn't love me, and I grew angry and suspicious. A man once said to me, when he was asking me to marry him, 'There was a time when I hated you because so many other men loved you, and because you made so many men suffer. I hated you the more because I knew that, if I came near you, I should love you too, just as blindly and irresistibly as they did. I made up my mind that I would steel myself against you, and make you love me, just as hopelessly as men have loved you, and then, when I was ready, I would turn my back on you as heartlessly as you appeared to turn yours on them. But your simplicity, where I had expected to find arts and wiles, disarmed me too completely, and this is the result.'

"That gave me a new point of view; but, Alice, I never had anything to terrify me so much in all my life. To think that a man, a great, strong, grown man, who had nothing against me but the fancied wrongs of other men, should have planned in cold blood the wrecking of my life—for if he had succeeded I should have gone straight to the devil, *nothing* could have saved me—fairly froze my blood with fear. I felt that instead of expecting any man to be my friend, I must regard every stranger as a possible foe. And this thing crept into my mind when Max acted so curiously. Oh, it shames me unspeakably to think that I ever could have allowed it to enter a heart which pretended to love such a man as Max!

"But the trail of the serpent was even there, and I looked at it until it grew familiar, and then I acted on the suggestion. I grew revengeful. I vowed that if he did not already love me, he should come to it; and if he did love me, he should tell me so.

"I put my own feelings entirely out of sight. And I made myself just as attractive to him as I possibly could. I grew reckless, and encouraged him and lured him on, because it was exciting and different from anything I ever had encountered before, and because I didn't care what the consequences might be. I let the future take care of itself.

"I could see that he was puzzled and surprised,

but attracted. Wherever I led, he followed, but in silence. His resistance made me even more determined, more eager, until one day I wrung the truth from him, and he asked me to be his wife. He said he never had meant to tell me, but I knew that I had made him, and when he told me *how* he loved me, and that he had loved me from the very beginning, I grew ashamed and frightened at discovering for the first time what it was to be loved by a man, a real man, not a make-believe or a beast; a man who never had loved anybody but me, who was no gallant to sigh at the feet of every girl, but who loved me in the old-fashioned way, which, if I were not such a worldling that I have grown ashamed to regard love as sacred—that's what the world does for one, Alice—I should say had something holy about it.

"I thank Heaven, as I look back, that I had enough of the eternal in me to reverence it and accept it and to return it in a degree, although I was not able to return it in kind, because I had had too many affairs before. I only wish now that I had been enough of a woman to be honest with him, and to give him the comfort of letting him know how I did love him. But I had the coquette's idea of keeping a man's love by withholding the full expression of it—of never saying that which he most wanted to hear. And although Max poured his whole honest, faithful soul out at my feet, he never knew how dearly I loved him. He knows it now.

"Once you asked me why I loved West Point. It was because I fell in love with Max there. He wore the cadet gray. He walked with me down Flirtation. He danced with me at the hops, and once they serenaded me with 'Benny Havens,' just as they did you.

"I think I am foolish for going year after year to a place which harrows me up and nearly kills me with its memories, but every inch of the ground is dear to me. I love every bugle-call, which used to mean so much to us. As I look back, Alice, it seems that I have lived and died by bugle-calls, for they signalled all our little engagements with each other, which were so short but so dear to both of us, held sometimes at the most inconvenient hours; and it was the bugle which said whether we could be together five minutes or an hour; and I loved it until once it played 'taps,' 'out your lights,' for the last time over Max's grave. The lights went out for me then and forever.

"I wish I could remember where I first met him. I am so jealous of every memory, now that he is dead, that I would give anything if I could remember every idle word, and all the jests, and little half-quarrels, and the joy of 'making up' in those days, before we knew that we loved each other. He is so much to me now that it seems as if I ought to have felt him coming, and known him out of all the world. *You* know where you met Gordon. You remember the first time you touched his hand, the first look he gave you. Whatever else you lose, you will always have that memory. Do you know these lines?

> "'I wish I could remember that first day,
> First hour, first moment of your meeting me,
> If bright or dim the season, it might be
> Summer or winter for aught that I can say,
> So unrecorded did it slip away;
> So blind was I to see and to foresee,
> So dull to mark the budding of my tree,
> That would not blossom yet for many a May.
> If only I could recollect it—such
> A day of days! I let it come and go
> As traceless as a thaw of by-gone snow,
> It seemed to mean so little, meant so much.
> If only now I could recall that touch,
> First touch of hand in hand—did one but know!'

"When you take up a book of poetry with such verse as that in it, Alice, you only half read it, no matter how carefully you look at each word. But when you trip over it by accident, and you have lived it all out in your heart beforehand, and the poet has only put your soul into words, *then* you not only are reading it—you are living it.

"Max was not brilliant, but I was desperately ambitious for him, as I am for myself and for you and for every one I love—ambitious to make the most of every opportunity, and to wrest from life all that it has to offer. So you can imagine my disappointment when he suddenly resigned from West Point to obtain a business position. For a long time I did not know why. Then I discovered that it was to enable him to offer me more. He never told me. I accidentally discovered it from something he said, and I never let him know that I knew, for, while I was touched beyond words to express, my disappointment was so bitter at his not understanding me better that I dared not trust myself to speak of it to him.

"Quiet men, men who are not brilliant themselves, always love women like me, and while doing their plodding best, sometimes misunderstand us lamentably. He never knew that distinction would be infinitely more to me than wealth. I cared nothing for what I was born into. My ambition reached out towards the unattainable. But when he made the sacrifice, mistaken though it was, and made it so gladly because it was for me, how could I explain it to him? I did not understand his heroism even then. I had to have a harder lesson to teach me to have faith in humanity. He always comforted himself by his belief that his younger brother would distinguish himself in his stead and win a higher place than Max could ever have won. His brother was the clever one, and Max idolized brilliancy, as most silent men do.

"But Max in a dull, commonplace business was quite different, in the eyes of the world, from Max in the army. The world said I ought to do better. The dear, kind, friendly world, which had done so much for me already, which had transformed me from an impetuous, hopeful, believing girl into a suspicious, calculating, worldly woman, stepped in and said it had predicted a brilliant match for me, and shook its head with a smile—the hateful, patronizing, sneering smile of the world at the rural idea of *any* genuine emotion—over Max's pretensions to my hand. *My* hand! Alice, I am telling you honestly, and you know humility is not one of my virtues, when I say that, to compare the cleanness of my hand with his, in the horrible clear light of Absolute Truth, I was not worthy to be his wife. I was frivolous, selfish, a flirt; and if I am anything else to-day it is because I have lived since by his life. Whatever I am, I owe to him.

"I said a moment ago that the world said I ought to do better. It was the world, largely in the person of my father. I will speak no harm of the dead. The best I can say of him, and I believe this is the truth, is that he did not know how genuinely Max loved me, and I was too proud—too wicked, I call it now—to let any one, even Max himself, know how much I loved him. Oh, what a mistake coquettes make! If only I could have him back for just one hour, I would trample my pride and my vanity and my worldliness under my feet, and I would give him, to his heart's content, the comfort I never once gave him then, of letting him know that I loved him with all my soul, as I love him now, and as I shall love him till I die.

"My father couldn't have known this, could he, Alice? No man could have been cruel enough to ridicule what we felt for each other, could he? But, oh, he said so much, and he was so clever with it all! I was proud and sensitive, and I pretended not to care. But his words cut, cut down into the quick of my foolish vanity, until I shiver and shrink even yet at the memory of certain phrases he used. He did not know what he was doing. Oh, he could not have known!

"But I was almost desperate, driven to bay; and when the war broke out, and Max raised a company, I was actually glad, for I thought that here was an opportunity for him to distinguish himself, as I was sure he would.

"Max gave up his business as cheerfully as if he already had not sacrificed one of the desires of his life to attain it. 'Duties never conflict,' he used to say to me when I rebelled at hard things. Ah, but he was a hero!

"He wanted me to marry him before he went. There was where the fine simplicity of his nature came in, which I was too poor in spirit to respond to. When once I had persuaded him that the obstacles which had kept him from speaking had been removed, he believed so utterly in my truth that he never gave them another thought. He took me at my word, and believed my nature to be as elementary as his own. It was not all my fault, Alice. Most men are unworldly naturally, and Max was the most unworldly of them all. But, oh! the world is a power which women feel in the most deadly way. We are complex enough to recognize its influence, but we never can make our position understood to a man. He frankly turns his back on it and says to a woman, 'I want *you*, and that's all there is to it.' But it isn't. Oh, but I'm sick of these distinctions! I am sick of my woman nature. I should love to be primitive, and broad, and daring, as men are. I would use my liberty to better advantage than they do. If I wore no fetters I would show people that it was because I did not need them.

"That was the sort of man Max was. But I could not explain myself to him, and, Alice, my hesitation was not *all* base. It was partly jealousy for him. I wanted him to win distinction, so that the world would be obliged to say I had done well. I wanted them to appreciate him—to see him with my eyes. That's what women like me have to do for the quiet, unassuming men who love us.

"So I held off, and promised to marry him when he came home. I told him to do something great, something to make me proud of him. I tried to appeal to his ambition; but it was pure patriotism which made him go and fight for his country. Then I tried to prick his vanity, but he had none.

"I never shall forget the way he looked at me. He was so big and tall, and had that kind way of looking down that most big men have—the protective look, brought out by a woman's smallness of stature. Max was so tall that even I seemed little beside him.

"I knew he was thinking of how I had encouraged him to love me, and had myself broken down all the barriers his pride had erected between us, and that now I refused to give him his reward—I refused to live up to my noble sentiments, only he wouldn't hurt me by saying so. He only squared his shoulders and drew a deep breath and looked over my head at the opposite wall, while I stammered and fluttered, not daring to speak out, and let him despise me.

"So he went away. He never reproached me. He only turned at the door and looked back at me, as Lohengrin looks at Elsa when he is leaving her and says, 'Lebe wohl.' He loved me, faults and imperfections and worldliness and weakness, too much to lay a feather's weight upon my happiness. But I have thought since that he believed in me and forgave me in spite of appearances. Max always did that. When I used to make speeches to people which were too daring or too wicked for conventionality, and instinctively looked at Max to see if he disapproved, he always forgave me by a look before I could even ask, and always put the best construction upon everything, and said I didn't mean it, and believed the very best of me always. Oh, Max!

"So he went away. I never saw him again. He was killed in his first battle, trying to rally his men. They were in a panic and it was no use. But if he had succeeded, it would have saved the day. They told me that there never was a more desperately heroic attempt made than his. He forgot himself. He never thought of danger. He was like a lion when he was roused, and he was killed trying to make his men die like men. But they were mad with fear and almost rode him down.

"He did nothing brilliant, Alice, dear. He neither saved the day nor obtained any glory. He simply gave up his life doing his duty as Max would do, only regretting that he had not succeeded better.

"He lay where he fell for hours, wounded fatally. And when they finally came to carry him from the field, he knew that there were scores of others who could be saved, so he refused to go. He must have lain there nearly all night, suffering alone. When they came in the morning they found him there, dead. And in his hand was a picture of me, but it was held so tightly that they had to bury it with him. I am glad they did. I am glad my face is where my heart is.

"That was my hero, Alice. That was Max Counselman, Gordon's brother."

As Kate ceased speaking, Alice gave a little cry and leaned her cheek against Kate's flower-like face in a silence too deep for words. So they held each other closely and clung together as women do, looking out over the river with unseeing eyes. Then it was that Alice realized that perhaps in this lay the message of her life, and that here and now she had come to her soul's cross-roads.

XI

THE BATTLE OF STOCKBRIDGE

STOCKBRIDGE society was quite stirred up over the arrival in town of three noted personages, who became, as was only proper and right, the personal property of the Copelands and Overshines. One was Senator Cobb, of Washington, whom the Stockbridge *Conservative* ineffectually tried to interview on the approaching election as he stepped off the train, but who expressly stated that he was here on private business, in so embarrassed a manner that the reporter, who was an astute young man, went back to the office of the *Conservative* and wrote up the senator's career, ending with the announcement of his engagement to the lovely daughter of one of our esteemed and leading citizens, leaving the name blank, and then held it over to await developments.

The other two arrivals were John Vandevoort, of New York, and Second Lieutenant Gordon Counselman, of the Third Artillery, who were guests of the Overshines.

Gordon arrived in the afternoon, and found Miss Vandevoort waiting for him with such a radiant face and in so bewitching a gown that Mollie Overshine, in spite of her vehement admiration for Kate, strongly disapproved of the way Kate was leading that poor young fellow on. She kept an eye on Kate every minute. Not a vivacious movement of that brilliant young woman escaped her; not a tone of Gordon's voice, pleading with her for something, which Kate was wickedly but laughingly denying him. Mollie was really vexed with Kate. "The girl has no heart," she thought. It was only the judgment of the world upon appearances, and no more severe and no more unjust than many another verdict of society upon circumstantial evidence. It is only by knowing the under side of things that we are able to judge brilliancy gently.

Miss Vandevoort was far too clever to allow Gordon to rush to call upon the Copelands the moment he arrived. She counselled patience both on account of reason and diplomacy, and Gordon was obliged to admit the correctness of her advice.

The lawn at the Overshines was deep and soft and velvety. Kate had inaugurated really comfortable rustic chairs, instead of the terrible back-breaking combination of slats and knots with which many excellent people strain the Christian forbearance of their guests. This simple *coup d'état* transformed it for the delightful afternoon hours into an out-of-door drawing-room. Mollie's tea-table and Kate's work-stand, a foolish but attractive little thing, just the kind of a three-legged affair that men ridicule and secretly admire, and always tip over, stood within easy reach, and here the children adored to come and talk and be laughed at and spoiled.

John Vandevoort, a taller, grander, gentler edition of Kate, sat watching Peggy, toiling and perspiring over her drawing. Peggy had few talents. She had to dig and delve for the acquirements which Frances fluttered over and knew without looking at. Frances was all sentiment, imagination, and superstition. Peggy was slow and practical and utterly reasonable. Her round eyes bulged out in wonder at the caprices and mental flights of Frances, who, much to her disgust, could never drag Peggy upward, nor even inspire her with a desire to soar. Metaphorically speaking, Frances always wanted to take the middle of the road, with plenty of elbow room, and Peggy admiringly stumbled along some distance behind, bravely swallowing her sister's dust.

"I wonder if all that grown people tell children about dying is true," said Frances, pirouetting about her father and Kate and the others, in a smart frock and scarlet shoes.

"I think so," said Colonel Overshine. "What, for instance?"

"Well, is it true that somebody is dying somewhere in the world every minute of the day and night?"

"Yes, that's true."

"My! Heaven must be an awfully big place. It must be bigger than the world, or it couldn't hold them all."

Peggy looked up from her drawing, and, pushing the hair out of her eyes, said judicially, "Well, I don't know, Frances. You must remember that hell takes care of a good many."

Colonel Overshine exploded. "Orthodoxy forever!" he roared.

"Don't laugh at them," said Kate, biting her lips to no avail; "it spoils them."

"Then why doesn't it spoil you, Aunt Kate, when people laugh at everything that you say?" asked Frances.

"It does," answered Kate. "I am dreadfully spoiled, Frances. I'm perfectly horrid, I think."

"Vous êtes une ange!" cried the child, impetuously casting herself into Kate's arms.

Peggy saw nothing in her remark to laugh at. She got up from the grass and smeared her warm red face with her dirty little hand. She looked at her drawing critically, not with her head on one side as Frances would have done, but straight ahead, with her round eyes glued to the picture. Then she made her way slowly over to Colonel Overshine, and sidling up to him, she said, politely:

"Cousin Chris, I've drawn a picture of you. The upper part is a very good likeness, I think, 'specially the whiskers. But I had to put skirts on you. I hope you'll excuse me, because I don't come to trousers until my next lesson."

They all coughed. Peggy would have been much hurt if they had laughed at her work.

"Hum, hum!" said Colonel Overshine, burying his red face in his handkerchief. "Very good, indeed, me dear. And as you say, the whiskers are uncommonly like. But—er—put me into trousers as soon as you can, me dear; I feel more at home in them."

"Oh, certainly. I forgot, when I began, that I wouldn't know what to do about your legs. I just happened to think of skirts when I saw Cousin Mollie sit down by you. I should like to draw Frank. He has been very kind to me. Do you think he would mind not having any legs?"

"Not at all, me dear. Frank being me own son, I can speak freely, and say he is one of the most accommodating boys I ever saw. If you have no use for his legs, Peggy, let him go without. The young fellows of to-day have too many luxuries, anyhow."

Frank Overshine was one of those amiable, well-meaning boys who, with the best heart in the world, always did everything wrong. He was slow, good, and exasperating. He always lost trains, and lost boats, and lost everything but his temper. Kate made fun of him unmercifully, but he adored her in spite of it. She called him "the late Frank Overshine," at which he only smiled deprecatingly. He was always planning reform. He was always turning over a new leaf. But he lived in the land of to-morrow. His intentions, however, were good, only Kate said he spent the most of his time paving hell. And that saying almost shocked several members of first families into untimely graves. Stockbridge never entirely approved of Miss Vandevoort after that, which gives you a very good idea of Stockbridge.

"I've just been out to see the Copelands," he announced, genially. But as he generally had just been out to see the Copelands, this surprised no one. Nevertheless, they all listened with more or less interest.

"How are they all?" asked Mr. Vandevoort. "I thought of going out there this evening."

"Mrs. Copeland sent word that she hoped to see you very soon. I told her that Mr. Counselman was here, too, and she said she was sorry George was not in town."

Kate smiled wickedly.

"Senator Cobb is there, I believe?" she said.

"Yes, he is there now, but he is going on the early train to-morrow. He wanted to go to-night, but Mrs. Copeland wouldn't let him."

"Why, how sudden!" said Mrs. Overshine. "I thought he meant to stay several days. I was going to entertain him."

"He got a telegram," said Frank, innocently, "calling him back at once."

"Then we ought to call to-night," said Colonel Overshine.

"Suppose we all go," cried Kate.

"All right," agreed Frank, with unnecessary promptness.

"How many times have you been there to-day already?" asked Kate, mischievously.

"Only twice. But Mrs. Copeland sent word last night that she wanted to see me." Frank involuntarily buttoned the top button of his coat and sat up straighter with the importance of this announcement. Mrs. Copeland generally treated him with a silent contempt, which the poor fellow never saw nor felt. But his mother saw it and felt it and resented it.

"How is Alice?" she said, kindly, in order to

give him an opportunity to speak of her. He was her only son, and she could not help wanting to lift him over the hard places.

"Why, mother, I don't know what is the matter with Alice. I never saw her stirred up so," he said, with more animation than he generally displayed. "You know how gentle and sweet she is, and how she never loses her temper? Well, when I was telling her what Cousin Kate had planned for the week while John and Mr. Counselman were here, and said, of course, she was to go everywhere we went, and all that, she almost stamped her foot —at least I saw it move—and she said her mother wouldn't let her go, and that she had to dress ninety dolls this week for that fair the Presbyterian church is going to have."

"Ninety dolls!" cried Gordon Counselman.

"Ninety dolls!" exclaimed everybody else in a breath.

"Oh, I wish they were all for me," said Frances, modestly.

"Why, I thought Alice had the candy table," said Kate.

"She has. This doll table is a new idea."

"It will be in her mother's name," murmured Mrs. Overshine, "but, as usual, Alice will do the work."

Kate frowned abstractedly for a moment; then

she wandered aimlessly over to Frank, and under cover of the general conversation she said, in a low tone: "What did Mrs. Copeland want of you this morning?"

"She said she sent for me to know if John Vandevoort had come."

"Was that all she wanted?"

"Yes, I think so."

"She didn't mention Mr. Counselman's name?"

"Not that I remember."

"Did you?"

"Oh yes; I told her he was coming this afternoon."

"Did you see Alice?"

"Yes."

"Did she say anything about the dolls then?"

"No; she seemed in unusually good spirits. It was this afternoon she told me about them. Isn't it too bad she can't go?"

"Can't go! Wait and see if she doesn't go. Is Mrs. Copeland the Pope of Stockbridge? I never saw anything so undisputed as her sway," cried Kate, indignantly.

"I never thought of it at all," said Frank, honestly.

"Of course not. Therein lies the secret of her power. It takes alien eyes to discover a despot so skilled as Mrs. Copeland."

"Don't let anybody hear you say that," begged Frank. "It might get you into trouble. We have to be so careful what we say."

"Thank Heaven I do not live in a small town!" cried Kate, raising her arms above her head. "Stockbridge would kill me in a year. I can't breathe here. It may suit the children, and it won't hurt them; but, oh me! the fetters on my spirit!"

"Well, I don't know about the children. I imagine that they misbehaved yesterday—in fact, had a regular scrimmage. Suppose you ask Hortense."

Neither Frank nor any one else ever thought of referring the children's discipline to their father. He was quite helpless before them, and perhaps none of the family realized this unfortunate fact quite so poignantly as those astute young persons themselves. They treated him like an adored bachelor uncle, who was always giving them presents, and in return got bullied, confided in, ignored, consulted, and tormented by turns, but never minded. Everybody took a hand at managing them except their father, or, rather, everybody avenged his or her personal affront on them, and the result of this go-as-you-please system was that they were as they were.

Kate was the only one who had a conscience

about them. She always treated them with respect and confidence, and they returned the compliment with the unstinted fervor of childhood.

"I prefer to ask them. They will tell. Frances and Peggy, did you have a nice time yesterday with Elsie Copeland?"

"No, Aunt Kate, we had a horrid time," responded Frances, with cheerful candor. "I consider Mrs. Copeland a most unpleasant old party."

Colonel Overshine shouted.

"You said so yourself, Cousin Chris," insisted the child. "I heard you."

"Elsie is a very ign'rant girl," observed Peggy, gravely. "She is lots bigger than Frances, but she has never been anywhere. Just think of it, Papa, Elsie Copeland has never been anywhere except to Philadelphia. She's never been to Europe even."

"And she isn't half as far in her arithmetic as I am, and she didn't know what geography was."

"And when Frances laughed at her, Mrs. Copeland said Elsie never could study because she was always sick. That was what started it," said Peggy.

"Started what?" asked John Vandevoort, anxiously.

"The row between Frances and Mrs. Copeland. But I was in it, too," declared the child, honestly. "Because Frances was so mad she couldn't see, and, of course, she was talking in French, and Mrs. Copeland couldn't understand her."

"Frances Vandevoort," began Mrs. Overshine.

"Wait a moment, Mollie," said Kate. "Let us see how it began. What was the very first of it, dearest? Tell Aunt Kate."

"Why, it was my accidentally laughing at Elsie because she didn't know anything. I didn't mean to be rude. But I was talking to them all at the table. They have dinner in the middle of the day, and let children come to the table. Oh, I think Stockbridge is too queer and nice for anything!"

"Go on with the story," said Kate.

"Well, I was telling about Japan, and Judge Copeland was listening just as politely as possible. He is very nice, Aunt Kate. I like *him*. He said he had never been there, but he asked questions, and I was telling him about the jinrikishas, and I said to Elsie it was lots funnier and nicer than the geography says, and she didn't know what geography was. And I laughed. But I was sorry the minute I did it, because it made the judge's face get red. I suppose he didn't want us to see that his child didn't know as much as we did, and she is bigger than we are. I was just going to say I was sorry I laughed, when Mrs. Copeland said, 'You are a very rude little girl, Frances, and if you were not a Vandevoort I would send you from the table.'"

"Ah-h!" breathed Kate.

"Go on," said Colonel Overshine. "Then what?"

"Nothing for a minute," put in Peggy, slowly. "But you ought to have seen Frances. Her face got as red as fire, and then it got as white as the table-cloth. You know how she looks when she is too mad to speak. She looked as though she was going to cry, too. And that made me feel so bad and so mad at Elsie's mother that when she said that about Elsie being too delicate to study, I said she wasn't sick at all. It was just thinking so. I said she was as well as I was."

"Oh, Lord!" cried Colonel Overshine, burying his face in his handkerchief and rocking himself back and forth. "Those children will be the death of me. Oh, why wasn't I there to see this thing. Peggy, me dear, I'm going to take you to the circus. Mollie, I'm going to give the children a party."

"Hush, Chris. Go on, Peggy. What happened then?"

"Then Mrs. Copeland turned on Peggy," broke in Frances. "And she looked perfectly furious, and she said, 'Who said that? I know you have heard some one say that. Tell me who it was.' But it didn't scare Peggy a particle. She just looked stupid, the way she does when she wants to, and I hollered out, 'Don't tell, Peggy.' And Mrs. Copeland said we were the worst children she ever saw, and that if we were hers, she would whip us."

"Then Frances got down from her chair and threw her napkin on the floor and stamped on it, and ordered Mrs. Copeland to call Hortense to take us home. Only she didn't understand French. Then Mrs. Copeland said to the judge, 'What an awful child! Emily Vandevoort's temper. I wonder that poor John has not sued for a divorce instead of Emily, and long ago, too.' *Then* Frances was raging. She said, 'Don't you dare speak of my mother's temper, or of my father's getting a divorce. Your husband ought to get one from you. You wicked woman. You're worse than my mother.'"

"In French?" pleaded Colonel Overshine. "Don't tell me she said that in French?"

"Yes, and it's a good thing, 'cause Mrs. Copeland looked as though she could kill her," drawled Peggy.

"Oh, Frances, why don't you speak more English? Oh, Mollie, me dear, what a pity the old lady didn't get that."

"Oh, but she was in a fury!" Peggy went on. "It didn't show except in her eyes. But she started for Frances, and I thought France would run, the way she does from Mamma, but she never moved. Just stood still and looked at Mrs. Copeland. And she stopped and never touched her. Frances said,

'Ring the bell for Hortense.' Mrs. Copeland understood that, because she pointed. And when Hortense came, we shook hands with the judge, and said we had had a very nice time, and we kissed Miss Alice, and only bowed to the others, and came away without finishing dinner."

"We shook hands with Gifford too, Peggy," added Frances, calmly. "He is such a pleasant boy."

Mrs. Overshine never thought of referring the trouble to their father, who was but an anxious onlooker at the scene. But she turned to Kate.

"I think you ought to punish them, Kate. They have mortally insulted Mrs. Copeland. She will never forgive *me* for this. You see if she does. I really think you ought to take them in hand."

"What good would it do, with Chris going on like a maniac over them? Look at him now with Peggy. I tell you, Mollie, clever children have no opportunity to be good and gentle and polite with such an injudicious family as we are. Besides that, to tell you the truth, in my secret soul I'm glad the Czar of Stockbridge got answered once in her life for her impertinence."

"That is all right for you, Kate, because you don't live here. But after you go, *I*'ve got to keep on living here. And don't forget for one moment that Mrs. Copeland will take it all out on me."

"Poor Mollie. Well, let us hope that she will take into consideration that we are Vandevoorts," said Kate, wickedly.

Mrs. Overshine had too keen a sense of humor not to relax a little at Kate's irony. "Nevertheless, for the children's sake, you ought to punish them," she answered.

But Kate shook her head. She remembered the child's face as she left her.

XII

THE COPELAND TERRACE

IF Mrs. Overshine had been in Kate Vandevoort's confidence she never would have permitted her household to call *en masse* upon the Copelands, for no sooner had the families fused than a polite battle royal began between Miss Vandevoort and Mrs. Copeland, which could not fail to give the victory to Kate.

Miss Vandevoort had two ways of managing. One was to make the path so clear that the most obtuse could not fail of seeing it. The other was so openly to speak out and tell her plans that all the men and a few of the women would disclaim any idea of her being politic, and declare her the frankest creature in the world. The rest of the women raised their eyebrows.

If the latter were true, hers was the art which conceals art, for while Mrs. Copeland was monopolizing Mr. Counselman with an affability which was completely disarming the unsuspicious young fellow, and tempting him to think Miss Vandevoort prejudiced in her sweeping denunciation of this amiable lady, while he was thus effectually being separated from Alice, with no signs of any change being compassed, and Alice's face was growing longer and more disappointed every moment, Miss Vandevoort rose up from her chair and said:

"Mr. Counselman, have you seen that fine view of the Delaware to be had from the side terrace? But of course not. Judge Copeland, may I show your precious view to our two strangers? Ah, thank you. Alice, dear, bring Senator Cobb, and let us show them the most beautiful sight in the world!"

Youth and innocence beamed from her guileless countenance as she swept aside the ponderously adjusted machinery of her antagonist, and detached the helpless creatures who were powerless to help themselves. The senator, with his head down and his hands under his coat-tails, walking beside Alice, whose face openly betrayed her discomfort, plainly told to Miss Vandevoort the story of his rejection, even if she had not known it already from Frank Overshine's ingenuous recital.

In seating themselves on the boat-house steps, Gordon had no difficulty in placing himself beside Alice. He only needed half a chance; but no unwarned man is a suitable antagonist for a predetermined woman. Besides that, it is said that even Jove nods upon occasions; but if Venus ever did, the record has been lost.

In the half-light of the setting sun, which charitably did its best to conceal the pitiful lowness of the river, the tiny islands which had risen to view as the river sank, and the smallness of the stream which crept silently by where it once had flowed with a proud crest, no one would have taken in all the defects of the Delaware, had not Miss Vandevoort, with the Hudson in her mind's eye, waved her hand and said:

"Fine locality for a river, is it not, Gordon?"

"The poor Delaware," said Alice, softly. "I feel so sorry for her. She has done her best, but Fate was against her. She has only succumbed because she was obliged to."

"That is only why the most of us succumb," said the senator, bitterly. "Fate is against us all."

"I only wish some good heavy rains would stay the hand of Fate in our lives as completely as it would in the case of the river," said Gordon, cheerfully. "But I don't believe in Fate. Do you, Miss Vandevoort?"

"I don't know," she answered slowly. "I believe in something—I think I call it destiny. It is not quite so pagan."

"Oh, I wasn't speaking seriously," said Gordon. "Of course we all know Who orders our lives."

Miss Vandevoort turned her head away abruptly. How like Max to avow what he believed so fearlessly.

"Look up there," she cried, pointing. "See the red in the river, and the black shadows, and the silver haze on the opposite shore, and the purplish light on the trees. Isn't that a lovely picture?"

"What a beautiful, misty look it has," said Gordon. "It is like a Corot."

"Only in a Corot we call that haze atmosphere, but in Pennsylvania we call it malaria," said Kate. When she was deeply moved, Miss Vandevoort always was most frivolous.

She rose as she spoke, and stood looking at the river absently. Then she went farther down the steps and paused. She knew they were watching her. She knew they thought her absorbed in something she saw. But the truth was, she was trying to leave them alone so skilfully that they would not know they had been left. Lovers are delicate objects to handle.

Again she paused, and looked over her shoulder at Senator Cobb. It made him think she wanted him. He had no idea that Mr. Counselman was interested in Alice, or possibly he would not have been so amiable. He merely thought, as Gordon was in the way and he could not see Miss Copeland alone, that he might as well follow Miss Vandevoort. She always amused him. That was one reason why most men were willing to follow her. She always amused everybody.

"I love Miss Vandevoort," said Alice, impulsively, as they watched her retreating figure.

"Do you?" said Gordon, smiling. "I believe I almost do myself. I owe her a great deal. It was she who obtained my appointment at West Point. I had no influence at Washington, but I was appointed by the President. My brother Max hoped to be able to manage it, because he was ambitious for me. You know Max was engaged to Miss Vandevoort, and I think that is the reason she has never married. She is a great belle, and always has been. I have heard my mother say that Miss Vandevoort could have occupied almost any position she wanted, so many really superior men have been in love with her. I suppose it is true—women know so much more about those things than men. I know the fellows at West Point go crazy about her every time she comes there. She never has been the same since my brother's death. I tell you, Max was a fine fellow. The sweetest thing about Miss Vandevoort is the way she has done so many things that Max intended to do. Now she knew Max wanted me in the army. And one day

she said to me, 'Would you like to go to West
Point?' Before I thought, I said, 'I'd rather go
there than to do anything else in the world.' That
was all. She just smiled. We never spoke of it
again. But she was a great friend of the President's,
and visited at the White House every winter. The
next year I was appointed. That's the way she
does things."

"It is just like her," said Alice.

"Yes," said Gordon, "it is just like her. Do you
know, even yet I can't get used to thinking of Max
as dead. Whenever I see Miss Vandevoort I think
he ought to be there with her. She never talks
about him, but once, when we had a long conversation after somebody had worried her with their gossip, she said, 'Knowing your brother has put other
men out of the question for me.' I wish that he
could have lived—for her sake. Still, I suppose it
isn't right to say such things."

He broke off abruptly and shook his head, as he
always did when anything bothered him.

There was a silence between them for a moment.
Then Gordon said:

"I never was so glad to see any one in all my life
as I was to see you this evening."

"Were you? I hardly thought you would come
the first day you were in town."

Gordon laughed.

"I wanted to come this afternoon — I should have liked to come straight from the train, but Miss Vandevoort wouldn't let me."

"I suppose she thought it wouldn't have been proper."

"No, that wasn't the reason."

"What was it, then?"

"I am afraid to tell you."

"Perhaps I know already," said the girl, flushing. "I have done you an injustice in my thoughts, but —it was not my fault."

"You couldn't help it," he declared. "I don't blame you. But I couldn't write again."

"No," said Alice. "Certainly not. But—"

"But what?"

"Nothing."

Gordon reached out timidly and took her hand. Alice made a faint-hearted effort to withdraw it, then left it there, and for a moment they sat there in silence. Alice was frightened, but tremblingly happy. She felt that her secret was slipping away from her, and passing into the keeping of the one from whom she would have hidden it the most carefully; and yet she did not care. For the first time in her life she was indulging in an emotion unrestricted by anybody or anything. For the first time she was letting herself go. It had all the intoxication of a timorous daring to the little Quaker maiden. And when Gordon said, "I love you, Alice, dear," it sounded so natural, so exactly as if he had been saying it forever, that she smiled at him with all her heart in her eyes, and the gates of Paradise swung open for another pair of pilgrims from earth.

It was so delightful to go back to the very beginning and talk it all over, and to tell each other everything they had not dared to mention at the time.

"And you were the prettiest girl at the hop," Gordon declared. "I think you are the prettiest girl I ever saw."

"Oh, nobody ever called me pretty before," disclaimed Alice.

"Then I don't see where their eyes have been."

"But I shouldn't have liked it if they had."

"Well, I shall say it as often as I please, and you must listen, because I can't help myself. You never looked as lovely as you do to-night."

"To-night? In this old dress?" cried Alice.

It was the first time she had worn it, but being in love would breed coquetry in a vestal virgin.

"Nobody was ever so happy as we are, were they?" asked Gordon.

"I don't see how they could be. I never was happy at all before, so I am no judge of it."

"You never were? Why, I have been happy always. Not, of course, like this. But I have found the world beautiful and people good, and I've always had plenty to be thankful for."

"I have had all that," said Alice; "yet somehow I have always just missed happiness. The nearest I ever have come to it has been when my father and I have been studying or talking together alone."

"My dear little girl! I will give all the rest of my life to trying to make you happy. I hate to think that you have missed it all this time."

"I don't know what there is in the future," said Alice. "But I wish things would always stay just as they are now."

"Oh," said Gordon, laughing, "we would get tired of boat-house steps and summer evenings and the river view. *I* want to think of a home of my own, and you for my wife, and of your coming to the door to tell me good-bye when I go away, and of your meeting me there when I come back. I am stationed at Fort Hamilton, and I know you will like it there."

"I?" cried Alice. "Oh, you don't mean soon?"

"Why not? My position is secure. I know exactly what I have to offer you, and why need we wait?"

"My mother—" began Alice.

Gordon squared his shoulders.

"Yes, I know," he said. "I suppose she will want you to wait."

"I am afraid she won't—"

"Won't what?"

"Let me have you at all." Alice blushed violently over the temerity of that speech, but the darkness was friendly.

"Oh, but she must!" said Gordon, vehemently. "You have promised me. And I believe you."

"You may believe me," cried Alice. "She must not separate us."

Gordon smiled confidently.

Mrs. Copeland was not used to direct methods in anything. She delved and circumnavigated so much that frankness upset and hurry completely finished her.

Gordon came to ask for Alice the next day—the very next morning, if you please—and suggested being married in the autumn.

He found the judge first, and made his avowal so frankly, as if expecting him to understand why he could not help loving Alice, and his youth and honesty were so appealing, that the judge forgot for one moment his wife and the senator from Ohio, and gave his consent before he realized what he was doing.

Armed with this, Gordon, with slower steps, sought Mrs. Copeland.

She was sitting unsuspiciously in her morning-room, with her fancy work. Her manner when Gordon came in was almost cordial; but when he plunged at once into the heart of his subject, and she discovered what had taken place, her anguish and disappointment and hurt pride at being outwitted were so intense and so confusing that she took refuge in such pleading with Gordon not to marry Alice, not to rob her of her dearest, almost— now that she was about to lose her—her only child, that in an ordinary matter Gordon would have yielded. But coming as he did from a healthy-minded, normal family, it struck him as such an impossible proposition that he was obliged to make an effort to take her seriously. Mrs. Copeland watched his ingenuous face like a hawk from behind her handkerchief, and inwardly chafed to read in it only pity and kindness, but not a ray of indecision. Her pleadings were so anguished, however, that Gordon said:

"My dear Mrs. Copeland, I am very sorry. I can understand how you love Alice, because I love her myself. But—excuse me for saying so—you could not expect to keep her always."

"I do expect to keep her always. I want my child's love."

"You have that, dear Mrs. Copeland. And you always shall. I never saw a more devoted daughter than Alice is to you."

"Ah, but I have been a devoted mother. Don't forget that, Mr. Counselman. I want my children around me always."

"But George tells me that he is to live at home here after he marries Miss St. Francis, so you will gain a daughter for the one you lose."

"You are not a mother, Mr. Counselman—"

Gordon threw his head back and laughed.

"No, Mrs. Copeland, I am not."

"How can you jest, sir, upon so serious a subject."

"I didn't, Mrs. Copeland. It was you."

"I never jested in my life. Well, laugh away, young people. The time will come soon enough when you will weep."

"Then may I have Alice?"

"It seems to me that you are taking her, anyway. I have nothing to say about it."

Gordon looked a trifle hurt.

"I will do my best to make her happy," he said, looking down.

"There is very little happiness in the world, young man. If you look, you will see more heartaches than smiles."

"I don't look for the heartaches," said Gordon, honestly. "And I see the smiles without looking."

"Alice will not be happy with you long. The tears will come and they will come on your account. It is always so. The woman suffers; the man laughs."

"I *hope* not," said Gordon, vehemently. I am going to be good to Alice always. I hope you believe that."

"You mean it now," said Mrs. Copeland.

"May I see Alice?" asked Gordon.

"I don't know where she is," she answered, without looking up.

"Then I'll *find* her, if you will allow me."

She did not notice his leave-taking, or see his proffered hand. He looked unusually tall and broad-shouldered as he walked away.

He found Alice down by the boat-house, and took her in his arms without a word. Alice read his face and asked no questions. She knew that he had conquered, and she guessed at what he had undergone.

"Alice," he said at length, "I wish you knew *my* mother."

XIII

ALICE'S WEDDING-DAY

For the *dramatis personæ*, a marriage engagement is an uncomfortable contrivance in many ways. Like the misunderstood honeymoon, it is easier for an outsider to weave romances about its perfect bliss than it is for the courageous participants, who are simply trying to live it down.

If you are engaged to a man of wealth and station, you have to fight to make people believe you love him—if you really do. If you are engaged to a poor man, when your fond relatives had predicted a brilliant match for you, you cannot even take the comfort of throwing yourself heart and soul into your trousseau, because you have to stop now and then to dangle your love for your *fiancé* before their eyes, in order to assure them that it will stand the stress of economy. So that there is no balm in Gilead.

Mrs. Copeland made Alice's a period of mourning. It so nearly shattered her always frail constitution that she never was a well woman afterwards. All Stockbridge knew this, and marvelled in her presence at the wonder and mystery of mother-love.

There are traditions of women to whom their engagement was the period of bliss for which books are the authority. But books are so misleading. There are other women who would not live through it again for anything—even to acquire the husbands whom its trials purchased.

Alice Copeland suffered an agony of apprehension through every hour of hers. She never knew at what moment the thread of her mother's patience would snap. She never was certain that Mrs. Copeland would let her marry Gordon. So many things conspired against her. Mrs. Copeland seemed to have taken a violent dislike to the army, and daily regretted that George was so unhappy as to be in its infantry service. It shows the superb discipline of her household that no one dared or even wished to mention the fact that she had sent him there against every one's wishes—even his own.

The several unfortunate things which had befallen army officers during her lifetime were rehearsed at breakfast every morning, Alice's only defence being that, at least, none of them had occurred recently, or to any member of Gordon's class.

But in reality, since knowing Mr. Counselman and discussing family trees with him, Mrs. Copeland had no more intention of breaking off the match than Alice herself. But neither Gordon nor Alice knew this. Gordon came to know the descent of the Giffords as well as he did that of the Copelands, which is saying a great deal. He once had been foolish enough, encouraged by a question of kindly interest from the judge, to offer a few facts concerning the Counselmans, and the not inglorious part they had played in the making of America's history. But he was met by such a roaring torrent —no, the mass was frozen and of majestic slowness—such an iceberg of ancestral history, proving the Giffords to have been descended directly from protoplasm, and each the most perfect lady and the most perfect gentleman of his time and kind, that Gordon was more than convinced that Mrs. Copeland was a lady. In fact, she admitted it herself.

When the preparations for the wedding ceremony were in progress, Alice was cheered in spite of herself. She knew that her mother's pride would allow nothing to interfere then. She even caught herself singing once or twice; but the reproachful look in Mrs. Copeland's face was sufficient to make her stop instantly, and to cling to her mother in a real and somewhat remorseful affection, to think that she *could* be willing to leave her for anybody —even for Gordon.

Two days before the wedding the papers were full of the suicide of Giles Pratt, Second Lieutenant of the One Hundred and Ninth Infantry. It was said to be a very sad affair, and a second great blow to the family, the first having been the failure of Mr. Pratt's father some three months before. The details of the unhappy affair were not made public, but something quite mysterious was hinted at.

Alice hardly breathed when she heard of it. She even thought of the daring idea of defying her mother, if Mrs. Copeland should pronounce this an impassable obstacle to her marriage. But Mrs. Copeland was a woman capable of lofty surprises. She glossed it over with a mental wave of her hand, which almost made Alice sick with relief, the revulsion of feeling was so great.

Of course Kate Vandevoort came down for the wedding. And so did her brother, because Frances and Peggy were to be flower girls, and strew the path of the bridal couple with the roses which Mrs. Copeland openly predicted would soon turn to rue.

Many guests came down from New York, and all the Giffords from Philadelphia came. Excellent people they were, with sterling principles and large bank accounts, and clothes four seasons behind the times. That was the Scotch of it—to buy good firm material which wore like iron, and then to wear it out.

There were people from Washington and Fortress Monroe and Fort McHenry and Fort Hamilton, where Gordon was stationed, and the first families of Stockbridge were there in force. There never was a prouder day for the Presbyterian church or for the Stockbridge *Conservative*, whose veracious chronicle of the brilliant affair is still preserved in the scrap-books of several maiden aunts who were there and who saw it all.

"Alice, my dear," cried Kate, who was maid of honor for the — but Kate declared she had lost track of the number—"fancy who is here?"

"Oh, I don't know. Tell me."

"Senator Cobb and his bride! Now try to imagine who his bride is. Mrs. Verry! Yes, honestly. I want to know if you ever in all your life heard of anything so delicious!"

"I think it is pathetic," said Alice.

"I came to help you dress. Let me do that for you. Are you nervous? Alice, that woman is a genius. The senator no more wanted to marry her than he wanted to marry his grandmother. But she made him think he did. Oh, but she is clever! I have always said that a man could marry any woman he wanted to—given equal conditions—and now I shall forever afterwards add that a woman can marry any man she wants to. Oh, what a dear, beautiful, funny old world this is!"

"I don't see how you can admire anything that Mrs. Verry does. I think she is horrid."

"Admire her! I admire her just as I admire Napoleon or Cæsar or Alexander—anybody who worked against fearful odds and succeeded. I may not admire everything about them, nor approve of all their methods, but I reverence their perseverance and their genius. Now, only I know what odds Mrs. Verry worked against, for I have heard Senator Cobb express his opinion of her, in days gone by, in no very complimentary terms. I am racking my brain to know what line of action she could have employed to change him and do everything up so speedily."

Kate paused a moment in deep thought. Alice thought her serious interest in this affair but another of Kate's whimseys. It was of no more moment to Alice than as if she had never seen Senator Cobb. But to Kate it was a problem which must be grappled with and solved before she could rest.

"You must admit that it is rather superb of her, Alice."

"How superb?"

"Why, to marry a man you discarded and show

him off at your wedding. It was a *coup d'état.* I thought I would warn you before you saw them."

"I don't see any *coup d'état* in it, and I didn't need any warning. I shouldn't care if all the men I know had married all the women I know and brought them all to my wedding. I shouldn't even see them."

"Oh, Alice, you are so queer."

"Have you seen Gordon since you have been here?"

"Yes, I saw him yesterday. I think that she touched his vanity. That is his weakest point."

"Whose? Gordon's?"

"No; Senator Cobb's."

"Oh! Did he tell you about it?"

"Did Senator Cobb tell me about it? Mercy, child, I haven't seen him."

"I meant Gordon."

"Oh no; John told me. They are on their wedding journey. They are going to Niagara. Gordon will hardly allow me to speak of it. I asked him yesterday if he had heard of it, and he said it was infamous. Now, what made him show so much feeling about it? Do you think it possible that Gordon was ever jealous of Senator Cobb?"

"No. No, indeed. He knows that I disliked him intensely."

"Then I don't know what made Gordon look so stern about it. There, dear, you look lovely."

"Thank you so much for coming to help me. I did not like the idea of dressing alone on my wedding-day. Mrs. Overshine came to dress me, but mother needed her the most, and I could get along well enough with a maid."

"You are an unselfish little thing, Alice. Tell me, have you got on

> 'Something old and something new,
> Something borrowed and something blue?'

That's for luck, you know. I always have to attend to my bride's luck."

"No, I haven't," said Alice, uneasily.

"What? Oh, you are reckless with your future, Alice. We must remedy that instantly. I never should dare to be married without."

"I chose Wednesday," said Alice.

"Of course. Wednesday is the only day for a wedding."

Both girls were quite serious, Kate half laughing at herself, yet conforming to the old rhyme. The most sensible women are superstitious about love affairs.

"Now, Alice, here is a pearl heart which Gordon's mother sent with her best love and the hope that you would wear it at your wedding. I know you did not intend to wear any jewels, but will you wear this?"

"Yes, indeed. 'From Gordon's mother!' Oh, Miss Vandevoort, don't you think I am the most fortunate girl in the world?"

"Yes, dear, and I hope you and Gordon will be as happy as you deserve to be."

Something in Miss Vandevoort's face as she was fastening the pearl heart in its place made Alice put her arms around her, in a sweet little way of hers, and whisper: "Dear Miss Vandevoort, you are so good to come to my wedding! It must be very hard for you."

Kate's lips quivered as she shook her head, saying: "Now, is there anything else I can do for you?"

"Nothing, except to leave me for a few minutes. I want to be all alone just before I am married."

Kate took Alice in her arms and kissed her. Then she went out and closed the door softly. She knew that Alice was kneeling beside her little white bed in her wedding-dress.

It was a military wedding. All the ushers and George Copeland, as best man, were in the full-dress uniform of the United States army. The bridesmaids were as pretty as newspapers always declare them to be. The ceremony was fifteen minutes late, as was perfectly proper—a ceremony

on time looks like quite indecent haste. Frances
and Peggy, who insisted on walking backwards in
front of the bride, as they once had seen flower
children do at a wedding in New York, had prac-
tised the difficult feat so successfully all their lives
that they performed their part with a self-possession and *savoir faire* which made Elsie Copeland
thrust her head behind her mother in their front
pew in vicarious nervousness.

Alice rose to the occasion in a wonderful way.
She was paler than usual, but she seemed to have
forgotten her surroundings. Kate, from the altar,
watched her progress down the aisle on her father's
arm. She fixed her eyes upon Gordon and walked
towards him as if on wings, forgetting where she
was, forgetting that people were looking at her and
whispering about her, forgetting everything except
that this was the happiest hour of her life, because
she never again was to be anything but Gordon
Counselman's wife.

Kate never could have lost herself like that.
Miss Vandevoort could love more deeply than
Alice, but she always kept her head. She always
knew where the hem of her gown was, and how
her train was hanging, and that people were looking at her. It was a subconsciousness, entirely
beyond her control and in no way interfering with
the deep experiences of her life, yet because she

talked about it people called her frivolous. Frivolity in women like Miss Vandevoort is but the casket enclosing jewels which only are shown to those who deserve to see their value.

The pause came, and the great hush, and the responses, and the shifting of figures around the altar, and the ring given and received, and then a burst of music, which announced that the wedding, the great event, was over, and Mr. and Mrs. Gordon Counselman were coming down the other aisle, with everybody turning and half rising to see their faces as they passed.

XIV

AT FORT HAMILTON

FORT HAMILTON faces the sea. From the officers' quarters you look across the immense parade-ground, bounded on two sides by the harbor and the ocean, and see the ships come sailing in, and watch with eager interest the coming and going of the little government steamers.

To Alice it was an enchanted land. She was sufficiently her father's daughter to love the glorious stretch of water which makes Fort Hamilton a blissful spot for those who love the sea, and Gordon was prouder to have secured a seaport station, because she seemed to love it so, than he was of his West Point record which sent him into the artillery.

Alice found herself facing a responsibility for the first time in her life. And though it was of the simplest description, she went on depending upon Gordon and asking his advice about the veriest trifles, just as she had been doing all her life with her mother.

Gordon knew quite as little as she, but he was

adaptable and self-reliant, and so supplemented Alice in quite a delightful and satisfactory way. One shudders to think what might have occurred had he been otherwise.

Except for all the other helpless women in the world who marry and go to housekeeping profoundly versed in ignorance of practical affairs, Alice would have been extraordinary in this line. Not that she had been idle all her life. Far from it. She had fetched and carried for her mother until it was second nature for her to thrust pillows behind people's backs and tuck footstools under their feet. And many persons unaccustomed to these gentle ministrations, who visited her in her new home, were so touched by her thoughtfulness that they cheerfully sat for hours with their knees too high for comfort, rather than reject her little props.

She played sweetly upon the piano, and the officers' wives at Fort Hamilton were glad to avail themselves of Gordon's voice and Alice's little tum-ti-tum accompaniments, which were so gentle and so seriously performed, and offered, as it were, with such a spirit of devotion before the shrine of her idol, that somehow it brought tears to your eyes to hear them. Or, if it did not go that far, perhaps it just made the bridge of your nose ache, which is the only stopping-place this side of tears for the pathos in the under side of things.

Alice, too, understood certain branches of cookery. She made delicious gruels and delicate custards, and when Gordon made fun of them, and expressed himself violently in favor of soups and roasts, Alice almost sighed to think how well and strong he was, so that she might never look forward to cooking her dear little messes for an invalid husband.

Mrs. Copeland sent Elsie down to visit Alice, and then this precious gift of sick-room cookery came so strongly into prominence that Gordon himself got a leave at the end of two months and took her home again.

"Mother does not like it because we did not keep her all winter," sighed Alice. "She said she thought the sea-air would be beneficial."

"So it would if either of you ever got any of it," answered Gordon. "But you never left the house for days at a time."

"I couldn't leave poor little Elsie."

"Then why didn't Elsie go out with you?"

"Oh, she didn't want to."

Gordon made no reply. He only began to sing:

> "Commentators tell us
> That when from earth we go
> We'll follow the same handicraft
> We followed here below.

> If this be true philosophy—
> (The parson he says no),
> What days of dance and song we'll have
> With Benny Havens, O!"

It was a whole year before Alice discovered that Gordon sang "Benny Havens" as an outlet for all the emotions that flesh is heir to. At first she thought he sang it because he was musical.

Alice importuned Miss Vandevoort in every letter to come and see their new home, but Kate held off on one pretext or another. "Wait until you get well used to each other's ways," she wrote, "so that you will not have to ask the bride-and-groom questions at the table which are so embarrassing to a person of my delicate sensibilities. At least, wait until you get used to each other's tempers. That will take a year. If you are not quarrelling at the end of a year, I will come."

But at the end of a year she would not come. She had spent most of the winter in Washington, and Alice wrote her an enthusiastic letter telling her of Gordon's promotion to be First Lieutenant, and begging her to come and celebrate with them.

Kate telegraphed them from Denver. She was with a party of her English friends in a private car, *en route* for California. She would come when she got back.

But it was two months after her return before she really came.

Alice was enchanted when she had Kate actually in her own home. She showed her everything. Kate could see that the house had been set in order as if for a guest of honor, and Alice had even robbed her own room to make Kate's more attractive.

Nearly all the officers in the post called the first evening she was there, and Alice never had seen Kate as brilliant as she was that night. She was almost too brilliant. She sang with Gordon and played with Alice, but there was something wrong with her wit. It sounded reckless to Alice. She kept watching the clock, and suddenly broke off what she was saying to Captain Fisher to dash into a spirited march which drowned conversation and set every one's feet to tapping with her marked time. But in the midst of it the bugle sounded "taps"—"Out your lights," "Out your lights"— and Kate's hands fell with a crash on the keys.

"Oh, don't stop!" they cried.

"She's forgotten the rest of it," said Alice, nervously. "She always stops there. She doesn't like the last part. I'll play for you."

"It is odd how so excellent a performer as Miss Vandevoort should break down in the middle of a thing like that," said Mrs. Fisher to Gordon. "It is her temperament, I think. She plays with a nervous tension. One of the most sympathetic and brilliant pianists I ever knew seldom managed to play a piece through. She nearly always broke down."

"Yes," said Gordon, watching Alice and Kate and wondering what was up, "I have heard of such things."

"Oh, they happen very frequently," declared Mrs. Fisher, thinking that her husband had been talking to that handsome Miss Vandevoort quite long enough, and deciding to go home at once.

Kate stayed one day more, then she told Alice she must go.

"I *can't* stay, Alice, dear. You know why."

Alice, who had been most importunate about her coming, helped her to make ready to go. Gordon was loud in his expressions of dissatisfaction.

"I thought you could put up with our little makeshifts longer than two days," he said, mischievously. "I am afraid you are what they call in books 'a spoiled beauty.'"

"I am just that," laughed Miss Vandevoort. 'Spoiled in the making."

"And it is because of your dear little makeshifts that I can't stay. They are driving me away," she whispered to Alice, as she kissed her good-bye.

"I am going back to Paris. One can forget everything real in Paris."

"She said I was changed, Gordon," said Alice, when Kate had gone.

"She meant improved. She told me so."

"She said lovely things about you, Gordon. But I don't need to have outsiders tell me how good and clever you are. I see it for myself."

"Oh, Alice, you would spoil a fellow. But I must say I would rather have my wife think me good and clever than to have everybody else in the world think so if she didn't."

Alice came and sat on the arm of his chair, and he pulled her fancy work out of her hands, and tossed it on the table.

"You don't like fancy work?" said Alice.

"I don't like to see *you* doing it. I would rather see you with a book."

"But I never read so much in all my life as since I have been married. And it has been lovely; lovelier even than to read with father. You are so interesting to talk with afterwards."

Gordon smiled at her derisively.

"No, now there is no danger of my spoiling you," she insisted. "You would have been spoiled long ago if flattery would do it. But you are so busy doing things for other people, and making fun, that you never seem to have time to notice what an attractive man you are."

"Am I an attractive man?" asked Gordon, solemnly.

"Very!" laughed Alice. "All the women are positively silly over you, only you never see it. You could have plenty of flirtations if you wanted to."

"By Jove, Alice, you are changing with a vengeance. I never heard you talk about flirtations before. It sounds too much like your friend, Mrs. Cobb."

"Not my friend, Gordon. Yours. She doesn't care that for the senator. She wants other men around her all the time."

"I don't see what people marry for, if they are going to keep on wanting attentions from other people. Why, the most wonderful woman in the world is not as attractive to me as my own wife."

Alice bent over and kissed him. She had not lost her old trick of blushing.

"How Miss Vandevoort would make fun of us if she could hear how silly we are," she said.

"It isn't silly for a man to make love to his own wife," said Gordon, stoutly. "This world would be a better place if more men did it."

"Miss Vandevoort says it doesn't last. She says it is the woman whom the man does not marry that he often loves the best."

"Miss Vandevoort's cynicism is the most amusing thing in the world when you know her. If ever there was a girl capable of making the sweetest wife in the world, except you, it is Miss Kate. But that sounds just like her. She only does it to cover how deeply she really feels. But she mixes me all up, she is so sudden and so brilliant. She addles my brain."

"Just as if anybody could do that," said Alice, fondly. "Tell me; was there anybody else in your case—anybody you didn't marry?"

"Anybody I didn't marry? Oh, yes; several. I only married you. I left a lot of girls for the other fellows."

"No, Gordon; don't joke. You know what I mean. Was there anybody you ever loved except me—anybody you ever think of when you sit and smoke with your eyes shut?"

Gordon flung his head back and laughed.

"Miss Vandevoort put that into your head," he declared.

"No, she didn't. It was Mrs. Cobb."

"Well, it does sound too decadent for Miss Kate. Her cynicism is more normal and healthy, and is always funny. Mrs. Cobb's is more like the trail of a serpent. I don't believe I care to have you see much of her, Alice."

"You are evading me," said Alice. "I asked

you a question and you are trying to get my mind off the subject."

"My dear wife, are you serious?"

"Yes, I am. I want to know if you ever loved any other woman except me?"

"Yes. I love another now. But it's my mother, I meant. Alice, child, how foolish of you to turn pale."

"I told you I was in earnest."

"Well, then, I will answer you. There is no one now, and there never was any other woman or girl in the world I ever wanted for my wife but you. I thought you knew that."

"Truly, Gordon?"

"Truly, Alice. I never loved anybody but you."

"Oh, Gordon, you are such a *dear!*"

"Now may I shut my eyes when I smoke?"

"Of course," said Alice, laughing, with a shamed face.

As Kate Vandevoort said, the Counselmans were so normal.

"Gordon, you are worried about something."

"How do you know, dear?"

"You sigh, and you are getting an up-and-down wrinkle between your eyebrows that only goes away when I rub it like that, and you shake your head this way."

"You have sharp eyes, little girl."

"Tell me what it is."

"Oh, it's nothing much. Just those debts. I hate to owe money."

"What debts, Gordon?"

"Those I told you about."

"Oh, yes. I remember. But you never told me what they were for."

"I indorsed a fellow's note, and he failed to pay it."

"Why couldn't he?"

"He died."

"Then it must have been Mr. Pratt. Tell me, was it Mr. Pratt?"

"Yes."

"I wonder what it was for? Mrs. Cobb told me a wife ought never to question any debts her husband contracted before he married her."

"Mrs. Cobb—" began Gordon, violently.

"Oh, Gordon, Gordon! What is the matter? What makes you look so?"

"Don't quote Mrs. Cobb to me, Alice. I—I—think it would be better not to."

"Gordon, how you frightened me. Sometimes I think you hate Mrs. Cobb. Why, even I only dislike her. What makes you, dear?"

"I think she is a wicked woman, and utterly without principle. I—I can't tell you what she has done, or how I know it. I hope there are palliating circumstances that I don't know of. Otherwise the injury she did a friend of mine I could hardly forgive."

"Oh, Gordon dear. I will never refer to it again. I did not know that you really had anything against her. Tell me about those debts. Do you owe any more than just what you told me about?"

"No, dear; that is all, but surely it is enough."

"But Gordon, only that little bit? Why, I can get you the money. My father will give it to me."

"Alice Counselman!"

"Well, he will lend it to me then, if you are so proud."

"Look here, Alice, I wouldn't have told you if I had thought you would suggest such a thing. You knew you were marrying a poor man, who could only offer you a soldier's pay."

"Well, have I ever regretted it or wanted anything different?"

"No, dear love, you have not. You seem happier here in this little house with nothing in it than you ever did with all the lovely things in that big house of your father's."

"Nothing in it? When you are here the whole world is in it for me."

"No furniture, I meant. I don't count myself furniture."

"Yet you furnish the house more than anything else," laughed Alice. "A sorry looking place it would be without you."

"Well, I come under the head of useless decorations, together with the parlor clock and your hanging baskets."

"Don't you make fun of my little house. I think it is prettier than any of the other officers'. And it cost so little."

"That's its chief beauty," laughed Gordon.

"It was your cleverness that did it. Would anybody but you have thought of having that little, old, crooked Japanese cabinet-maker make us a set of parlor furniture out of bamboo, and the whole thing costing less than one of the chairs in my room at home?"

"We don't mind if the sticks run into people's backs so that our company only stay a few minutes, or, if they come again, say they prefer to stand up?"

"Oh, it isn't as bad as that. Of course they are not the most comfortable things in the world; but who ever sits in a parlor, anyway?"

"Nobody."

"And doesn't everybody think those hammocks in the library are the most amusing and the queerest conceit in the world, and doesn't it put everybody at their ease immediately to sit in a hammock with anybody?"

"It does."

"Well, whose idea was that?" demanded Alice.

"Mine."

"Well, then, aren't you clever and nice and lovely, and am I not the happiest girl in the world?"

"You certainly are the most attractive to me. But listen now. Wouldn't you really rather have a nice set of black hair-cloth furniture for the parlor, with this good, slippery kind of a sofa, that you sort of skate around on without half trying, and a marble centre-table with a red-plush album on it to hold family photographs, and a case of wax flowers on the mantel, and a motto, 'What is home without a mother?' worked in green, to hang over the door?"

"Gordon, don't make fun of your brother officer! Perhaps they are just as happy eating from a red table-cloth, 'because it looks so cheerful,' as we are."

"Who is making fun now?" demanded Gordon.

"There, you sighed again. Are you really worried about that money?"

"It bothers me," answered Gordon, shaking his head from side to side.

"How funny. Well, how are you going to pay it?"

"I don't know. I'll find a way. I have several schemes in my head. I had thought of resigning."

"Gordon! You don't mean it? Why, I wouldn't have you for anything. Let's economize."

"You mouse! You don't know what economy means!"

"Yes, I do. I'll go without things."

"You'll go without a veil for yourself and buy something for me that costs ten dollars," said Gordon, pinching her cheek.

"Oh, you don't want me to economize on *you?*"

"I don't want you to economize on anything," sighed Gordon. "I wish I had a million for you."

"I don't want it," declared Alice. "I only want enough so that you won't worry."

"I have thought of applying for the professorship of Military Science in Colby University. How should you like that?"

"Oh, I should love it. And I am sure you would get it."

"What faith you have in me, Alice."

"Because I *know* you," she insisted. "But wouldn't it be some time before you could get it?"

"Yes, a year, at least."

"And you would worry all that time?"

"Well, I shall not be quite comfortable until I pay what I owe."

"Gordon, dear, won't you please, please let me get the money for you?"

"Alice, if you know some—just a few of the

things your mother has said to me, you would know how impossible it would be for me to accept the smallest favor from her unless you were suffering."

"Oh, dearest, I did not know! Please forgive me. How good of you never to tell me before. My poor boy. Well, we are *not* suffering, and we will starve before we will ask them for anything. Poor Gordon! You have borne so much for me."

"I'd bear a good deal more for such an angel as you are. Never mind, dear. I've never had money. I shouldn't know what to do with it. But I've got you and you've got me, and as long as God lets us have each other, we will be happy. Don't fret now. There goes 'tattoo.' Be at the window for me when I come back."

XV

THE FORK IN THE ROAD

DURING the first years of their married life letters came regularly from Mrs. Copeland imploring Alice to come home and smooth her mother's path to the grave. She knew that she had not long to live, she wrote, and would Gordon have the heart to separate them? Of course Gordon would not, so they both went down to Stockbridge, but Mrs. Copeland showed no signs of dying, and Alice so soon settled down into the little mouse she was before she was married, that Gordon promptly took her back to Fort Hamilton.

Three times were they summoned for this purpose and three times did Gordon quietly take her home with him, undergoing in perfect silence Mrs. Copeland's biting comments on his course of action. Only once he left her there, and when he came again, it was to see Alice and her little son—no longer the Alice he had known, but an Alice who had begun to take a hold upon the deep things of life.

Mrs. Copeland insisted that the baby was delicate from the first; and, in spite of Gordon's stout denials, Alice looked so frightened when her mother came into the room and pulled the curtains down and looked at the baby and shook her head, that although Alice had meant to stay in Stockbridge for a while, she was obliged to admit that Gordon was right when he insisted that she must come home with him at once.

"But I am so afraid something will happen to the baby without some one who knows more about children than I do," pleaded Alice. "Can't we have your mother to live with us?"

"Write and ask her," said Gordon, laughing, "and see what she says."

So Alice wrote a beautiful letter, in her neat, little round hand, and Mrs. Counselman wrote back that she would hold herself in readiness to come at an hour's notice, but that no house was large enough for two families.

"What did I tell you?" cried Gordon. "She knows."

"I suppose she is right," sighed Alice. "Every time I see her I know why you are so good, and when I see your father I know why you are so clever."

"I am deeply thankful that it can be explained by heredity, and that, unlike Topsy, I have not 'just growed.'" laughed Gordon.

"I hope Lloyd will be like you," said Alice, fondly. "Mrs. Fisher says he looks just like you."

"Oh, I hope not! I hope I don't look like that, Alice. I'm not conceited, but you know I am better looking than the baby."

"Now, Gordon, you can make fun of yourself, if you like, and you can make fun of me, but you shall not ridicule this precious child. Aren't you ashamed of yourself?"

"Yes, I am."

"Just look at him; he actually cries for you when you go away. Isn't he pretty?"

"Beautiful."

"And doesn't he look like you?"

"Exactly. If you put my clothes on him, you couldn't tell us apart."

Alice gave up in despair. Mrs. Fisher comforted her.

"All men talk that way, my dear. Wait until the baby is older, and then see what Gordon will say."

"Why, he is just in fun," cried Alice, indignantly. "He fairly adores him when we are alone. He likes to tease me, that's all."

No harm befell the child during his first year, in spite of Alice's constant worry. Gordon kept her away from Stockbridge, and gradually she came to believe that the healthful, merry little fellow, who really was like Gordon, would live, if they would simply allow him to breathe and sleep and kick in his own sturdy little fashion.

So the summer wore away and their third winter came. The changelessness of army life suited Alice perfectly, but its inertia preyed upon Gordon.

One day, when Alice stood at the window watching for his return, she saw him wave his cap at her from a group of officers standing in front of the Mess, with their arms on each other's shoulders and their heads together in a bunch, talking excitedly over something. They dispersed twice, and twice came together again, talking, talking, and gesticulating.

"What can it be?" thought Alice, wonderingly. "News from the War Department, I suppose. But why doesn't Gordon come and tell *me*?"

He broke away from them at last, gave his cap a jerk over his eyes, buttoned the bottom frog of his long overcoat, held the top together, and came up the steps at one jump.

"Great news, Alice!" he cried as he opened the door and caught her off her feet.

"Oh, *what* is it, Gordon?"

"Regiment is ordered away. We are going to move!"

"Oh," said Alice, her face falling.

"Oh, what a disappointed tone! Why, it will be

jolly. You don't know what fun it is to move. It gives a fellow something to do."

"I should think it would," said Alice, ruefully.

"Our company is ordered to Fort Jefferson— Dry Tortugas."

"Where is that?" asked Alice, with all a woman's charming ignorance of geography.

"One of the Florida Keys — off the southern coast of Florida."

"South? Florida? Oh, how lovely! I've never been South, and I've always been crazy to go. Why, to be ordered to Florida in winter is to have the government treat us like millionaires."

"Won't it be fun? We can wear thin clothes all winter, and in the summer you will have to come North."

"Well, I'll come home and visit, and you will spend your leave with us and that will break the summer for me. Then just as soon as it gets cool in Stockbridge we will follow you to Fort Jefferson."

"My goodness, how we shall want to see each other by that time, when I want to tear down to Stockbridge the day after I let you go," sighed Gordon.

"Florida will be good for the baby," said Alice, wisely. "Cold weather doesn't agree with him very well."

"Florida will be good for the bamboo furniture," said Gordon. "It won't be necessary to have it padded and steam-heated the way we do here."

"And the hammocks!" laughed Alice. "How considerate Uncle Sam has been of the Counselmans' furniture!"

"We can live in hammocks the year round," said Gordon. Then he began to sing:

> "From the land of sun and flowers,
>   From Tampa's lovely shore,
>   There comes a wail of sadness up:
>   O'Brien is no more.
>   The prince of all good fellows,
>   Ne'er a better do we know,
>   May we meet him in that happy land
>   With Benny Havens, O!"

He insisted upon beginning to pack that night, and by morning the whole post was upset. Alice was not used to such topsy-turvy haste, and at first it shocked her sense of the proprieties. But the other officers' wives were equally expeditious, and so plainly made it appear the only thing to do that Alice sensibly joined in, and soon was packing as crazily as the rest. Gordon was so big and strong and helpful, and made so merry over the hard work, that Alice spent most of her time laughing and following him around, holding the baby.

The Counselmans were ready first, of course. Gordon had rushed around to such an extent, and they were young, and had so little to pack, that long before marching orders came he found time hanging heavily on his hands. So he fell to helping the ladies of the post to do their part of packing bric-à-brac and clocks.

He did it so deftly and made such light work of it that the officers declared that Counselman spoiled their wives by too much waiting on them. But Gordon never could bear to see a woman do anything which looked hard. He had such a merry way of taking her work out of her hands, however, that they never realized how much he helped everybody.

"Oh, dear, why will people give us onyx clocks and bronze vases, when the government only allows us seven hundred pounds of luggage!" sighed Mrs. Fisher.

"Never mind. Pay the extra freight with a smiling countenance. You won't have so much next time. Three moves are equal to a fire, you know," said Gordon, soothingly.

"Isn't he consoling?" cried Mrs. Fisher.

Gordon insisted upon being paid by Welsh rarebits made in the chafing-dish and eaten from tin plates, with everybody sitting around on boxes, and of winding up every evening with a "sing." Sometimes voices broke and lips quivered over the dear old songs which, perhaps, they might never sing together again.

"I should be jealous of you, Counselman," said Major Prescott, who never did anything he could help doing, "if you took advantage of one-half my wife says of you."

"Your wife, Major, is one of the most charitably disposed women I know. She covers my shortcomings with that which 'never faileth.'"

"You think she 'suffereth long and is kind,' do you?" laughed the major.

"I think she is using me as an example to make you work," answered Gordon, confidentially.

The Third was to be very generally scattered along the coast. The officers were pleased at the prospect of a change which promised to be so pleasant, but Gordon Counselman, the youngest first lieutenant in the regiment, and the one assigned to the most unpromising post, was so much more pleased than all the others that he infected the rest with his spirits, and made the last days of the Third's stay at Fort Hamilton a jubilee that no one who participated ever forgot.

The discontented and the fretful and the chronic complainers were the ones he took especial pleasure in diverting, and the result was that, for so radical a move, it was the most harmonious the regiment ever experienced.

Those ordered to Pensacola and Tortugas, he claimed, were the most favored. He painted Florida in glowing colors, and insisted that "Fort San Carlos de Barancas," the name of the fort at Pensacola, sounded so Spanish and so Mexican and so foreign that to go there would be like a composite journey around the world, with Uncle Sam for a letter of credit.

He sent Alice and the baby down to Stockbridge on Friday, and he was to spend Sunday with them to say good-bye, bringing them back with him to sail on Monday.

"Your mother will say that you are looking pale, Alice," said Gordon, anxiously, bracing her to resist the mental malaria of her mother, "but you must tell her that the post surgeon says Florida will set you up and be the best thing in the world for you. And as to Lloyd, a warm climate is exactly what he needs. Now, don't forget this."

"I won't, dear. I will remember everything. Button up your coat. You will catch your death cold with it flying open that way."

Gordon obediently buttoned it. He thought it charming to be looked after in this way by his pretty little wife.

"Now let the nurse hold the baby. You needn't be afraid people will think it is hers."

"Gordon!"

"Well, you are apt to overtax yourself, and I must take care of you. You are looking a little pale."

"Why, Gordon, you are just like mother," said Alice, innocently. She never saw her mother with other people's eyes.

"Heaven forbid!" thought Gordon. But he did not say so.

They watched each other out of sight, as if they never expected to meet again. Nor did they suspect that any one noticed them or thought them either odd or foolish. But one or two women who had outlived the expression of their husband's love felt a queer little lump rise in their throats as they turned away.

When Gordon arrived in Stockbridge and tried to spring up the terrace steps as he did at home, he felt his feet drag in the old, unmistakable way. Although he never showed it, he disliked the house, the grounds, the whole place as only a proud man can where he has been insulted by a woman in scrupulously polite tones.

He found Mrs. Copeland in a pious state of resignation, and Alice with a face whiter than the baby's dress.

"What is the matter, dearest?" he said, taking her into his arms. "What are they tormenting you about now?"

"Mother says she is too delicate to be left alone, and that she will die if I go to Fort Jefferson. Oh, Gordon, Gordon, it will break my heart to be left behind."

"You shall not be left! I won't leave you! You are my wife more than you are your mother's daughter, and you shall go where you want to go."

"Oh, that would be with you, darling. But I really think I ought to stay. You can see for yourself that mother is failing."

"No, I cannot."

"Well, she is, and she needs me."

"Let George's wife take care of her. She is here all the time."

"Yes, but mother wants me, and she says my first duty is to her for the little time she will be on earth. If I went and she should die, I could never forgive myself."

"She won't die," said Gordon, gloomily.

"Poor mother. She is such a sufferer," sighed Alice. "I know that I ought to stay."

"Alice, do you really feel it your duty to stay?"

"*She* thinks it is."

"Well, use your own conscience. What do *you* think?"

"I think I ought to go with you."

"Then you shall go."

Alice clung to him in silence, with her face buried in his coat, glad to have him decide for her, and take the responsibility off her hands.

But it was a cheerless day. Alice stayed up-stairs with her mother in a darkened room; the doctor was called in, and Gordon and Judge Copeland smoked in the library and talked fitfully of everything except that which lay uppermost in both minds.

The Overshines came over in the afternoon to say good-bye, but they hurried away again from a house filled with such careful gloom.

When the doctor left, Gordon went to get Alice and take her for a walk.

"Gordon," she said, when she saw him, "It is no use. I must stay here. The doctor says Florida might kill my baby."

"The post surgeon thinks differently."

"Yes, but mother says Dr. Jamison knows my constitution, and the baby's, and that I will be running the gravest risk if I take him. I have decided. I must stay here."

Gordon said nothing. He was too bitterly disappointed to speak. He only took her in his arms, and kissed her and petted her all the rest of the time they were together, in a way which afterwards came back to her, as if, even then, he must have known.

If he felt that Alice was wrong he never said so, and she could not seem to feel intuitively that she had failed at the supreme test. Men like Gordon are braver than the Alices of this world ever know. She thought it perfectly natural that he should hover around her in an agony of love and tenderness, but which was largely disappointment—not in her; he was too loyal for that. But a great bitterness of spirit surged up and overwhelmed him at the cruelty of the unknown elements in her nature which made it impossible for her to meet him on his plane. Gordon was undergoing the mortal agony of a soul sick, sick unto death, and without the power of speech which might lead to healing.

Alice was sharing his unhappiness to the best of her ability. One has no fault to find with the purling river which runs into the mighty sea. Doubtless the river would feel more natural in finding its outlet in a lake.

She clung to him at parting with such soft, womanly tenderness that Gordon forgot some of the deep-searching pain he had undergone. But his face, which always was so merry, took on such a look of anguish when he held his baby son in his arms for the last time that Judge Copeland turned hastily away.

Gordon tried to go twice, and twice came back again, to undergo once more the sweet bitterness of pressing his face against the soft baby cheeks of the little fellow, who tried to understand what Alice was saying to him about dear papa's going away.

Gordon looked back from the gate, and Alice was at the window waving Lloyd's baby hand for him. Gordon was not ashamed of the tears which forced themselves to his eyes at the sudden mighty ache of his heart.

XVI

INTO SILENCE

GORDON COUNSELMAN had all a soldier's idea of duty. He followed his own conscience, and permitted everybody else, even his wife, to do the same. Although he could not upon this occasion quite agree with Alice in her point of view, still he defended her against every one who blamed her for not going with her husband, as many people dared to do. He admired Alice's devotion to a forbidding duty, which she paid so unswervingly. He doubted if, in her place, he could have done it so promptly. A man with a conscience will sacrifice his head and his bodily comfort to his ideal of duty, but he clings tenaciously to his heart's desire, and yields that last, if at all. A woman with a conscience often makes a burnt-offering of her heart, from pure altruism. Men call such a woman either a saint, or—cold.

To Alice's grief, she discovered that nearly everybody in Stockbridge, and, later, that even Miss

Vandevoort herself, thought her entirely wrong in her course of action. Some gave her no quarter. The kindest only said that her conception of duty was ill considered. Her letters to Gordon's mother, hitherto so affectionate, became constrained and apologetic; and Mrs. Counselman's silence upon this one subject in her kind replies grieved Alice beyond measure—it was so eloquent a condemnation.

It was part of Alice's inheritance, that in spite of all this she never thought of changing her mind and following Gordon to Fort Jefferson.

When it became too much to bear, she overflowed in her letters to Gordon, and he assured her that no one was competent to judge so well as her dear self, and he upheld her so courageously that she believed he wholly approved her course—so much so that she began to think, and to say to others, that in remaining in Stockbridge she was following her husband's advice.

When Kate, at Nice, received the first letter from Alice, in which she put this into words, it did not change her opinion in the slightest degree. She knew just how Alice came to believe that. She dropped the letter in her lap and sat looking out over the blue waters of the Mediterranean as if her eyes saw something from the long ago.

Little Lloyd was growing finely. He was one

person to whom Alice could talk of Gordon by the hour. She tried to make him an entity to the child. She filled her rooms with pictures of him, and made him the hero of all the wonderful tales she wove for the sleepy hour. She read his letters aloud to the little fellow, who listened with grave, intelligent eyes, and guided the baby fist in the hieroglyphics which went as replies from Lloyd to his papa. Alice even sent Gordon the photograph of himself, taken in his uniform, which Lloyd considered his. It was all blistered from the moisty kisses his little son had imprinted on the face in his bursts of affection for his soldier father, and Gordon laughed, with tears in his eyes, when he saw it.

Perhaps they were very foolish, these two young people. But they loved each other, and they went blindly forward, hoping for the future, the dear future which should bring them together.

The winter passed, spring came and went, and summer was half over. It was time for Gordon to have his leave. Alice was growing restlessly impatient. It was very hot in Florida, and had been summer with them when there was snow in Stockbridge.

Suddenly a letter came which almost repaid Alice for her year of separation. The long-looked-for detail as professor of Military Science at Colby University had arrived, and with it Gordon's leave of absence. That meant no more separations, no more debts, no more worry, and Gordon with her for at least four years. Alice almost ran to tell the good news to her friends. Gordon had saved it to surprise her. She talked to Lloyd until the child was nearly crazy with delight. Gordon's letter said that he might arrive at any time. Letters were so often delayed coming from Tortugas. "You may look for me at any hour," he wrote.

"Papa may come to-day, dear lamb," she cried to Lloyd. "Perhaps he is here now. Perhaps he is just getting off the train. Perhaps he is coming down the street. Let's look out of the window and see if we can see him. How big is he, darling?"

"Bigger dan g'an'papa," said the child.

"And what does he call my baby?"

"Papa's p'ecious little son."

"And what does my baby call him?"

"My darlin' foddy."

"And what are you going to do when you see him?"

"I'm don' tiss 'm, 'n' hug him much as I love him."

"Oh, you little angel! You remember it all. Now, you won't forget when you see a great big man, and I say, 'That's your foddy,' will you?"

"No," said the child, solemnly.

"Come, let's sit at the window and watch for

him. His letter said, 'At any hour.' Here, sit in mamma's lap, and let me brush your curls. Do you remember how we sent one of these curls to dear foddy, and he put it in the back of his watch, and a little hair got into the wheels and stopped them? Wasn't that funny? Oh, look! There comes a messenger boy with a telegram. Perhaps that is from papa, saying that he has arrived in New York. Let mother run to get it."

She opened the telegram without a fear. It was from the post surgeon at Fort Jefferson.

"Mrs. GORDON COUNSELMAN, Stockbridge, Pa.:
"Lieutenant Counselman died of yellow-fever on the 11th inst., at 5.30 P.M.   G. H. CARSON,
"Post Surgeon."

Alice fell just where she stood, like a broken lily. It was her father who found her, and with unspeakable tenderness carried her to her bed, where she lay crushed and helpless.

The blow had fallen so suddenly and with such mighty force that for weeks she remained in a dazed, semi-conscious condition, shedding no tears and making no outcry.

The doctor shook his head when day after day passed with no change. But nothing aroused her stunned intellect, nothing brought the healing tears, not even the presence and pitiful wailing of her boy, who could not understand why his caresses were unnoticed and unreturned.

When she grew strong enough to creep out into the light of day a letter came from Dr. Magnus, of Key West, who had gone to Gordon's assistance when the pestilence broke out at the fort.

She was sitting listlessly at the window, with her boy in her arms, when this letter was put into her hands to read:

"Mrs. GORDON COUNSELMAN:

"*My dear Madam*,—My telegram in answer to your inquiry concerning Lieutenant Counselman doubtless has been received. Some further particulars I now give by mail. During the violence of the epidemic at Fort Jefferson I volunteered my services to assist the medical officers at that post in the care of the sick.

"Upon my arrival I found the officers at the post, including Lieutenant Counselman, wellnigh exhausted with incessant watching and assiduous care of the victims. During my stay of some ten days no one displayed a more exalted sympathy, more zeal and anxiety in the care of the sufferers, day and night, than your husband, entirely forgetting and ignoring self in the discharge of self-imposed duties to those committed to his official care. The leave of the colonel of the regiment had expired some few days before, and Lieutenant Counselman's date for departure was therefore delayed. But although repeatedly urged to go, the nurses were too few for him to permit himself to listen to their generous suggestions. I remained with him until the epidemic began to abate, when I returned to Key West.

"Two hours after my departure from the fort, on the 8th inst., he was violently stricken down, and although a gun was fired and the flag displayed at half-mast, the vessel upon which I left was too far out for the gun to be heard or the signal of distress to be seen. He died after three days' illness, truly, sincerely, and deeply regretted by friends, acquaintances, and unusually so by his comrades.

"During the epidemic it had been the custom for the colored attachés of the post to bury the dead. But during the still hours of the night, after his death in the late afternoon, those of the soldiers who had volunteered their services as nurses and attendants, desirous of paying the last sad tribute to their beloved commander, whose last words were, 'I have stood by you,' secretly removed his remains, and buried him silently and tearfully, with their own hands, in an adjoining key some two miles distant.

"The surprise of the officers the next morning was great, but appreciating this portrayal of affection on the part of his soldiers, they were silent as to the breach of discipline, and proceeded with the plan of interment.

"They were rowed over to the key, and with appropriate services committed his body, dust to dust and ashes to ashes, and his soul to God who gave it.

"The loss of such men as Lieutenant Counselman is truly great, to home, country, and friends, and is a forcible example of self-sacrifice in devotion to duty.

"Hoping that this sad affliction to you and friends at home may be somewhat softened by your knowledge of the circumstances under which he was taken,

"I am, my dear madam,
"Very truly yours,
"JOSEPH MAGNUS."

When Alice finished she buried her face in her baby's little white dress, and fell into the bitter, bitter weeping which only the widowed know.

Then she took Lloyd in her arms and went and stood before a large portrait of Gordon. The baby looked wonderingly at her tears.

"Look there, my darling. There is a hero that nobody will ever hear about. Only you and mamma know that he gave up his life for other people, and that we are proud, proud that we belong to him and bear his name."

She took the letter down for her mother to read. Mrs. Copeland had been prostrated ever since the news arrived. Alice sat down by the window overlooking the Delaware and the boat-house steps where Gordon had first told her he loved her. She still held Lloyd in her arms.

Mrs. Copeland sobbed aloud over the reading of it, but Alice only rocked the baby back and forth, and looked out over the river.

"He was a hero, mother," she said, quietly. "Pray do not exhaust yourself so. I only wish that people knew how good he was. But they would forget, if they did know. You and I, Lloyd, will never forget. We will always remember him, won't we, baby?"

"Papa's p'ecious little son," murmured the child, sleepily.

Alice kissed him and smiled.

"Is my foddy tummin' to-day?" he asked.

"Not to-day, darling. Perhaps to-morrow."

"My foddy's tummin' to-morrow," he repeated, leaning his curly head against Alice's shoulder in sleepy content.

Judge Copeland came in and laid his hand tenderly on Alice's soft hair. It was so exactly Gordon's way and Gordon's touch, that she bowed over her baby's head in helpless sobbing.

"Are you able to read this, dear daughter?" he said. He handed her a newspaper, pointing with his finger to a column headed, "LIEUTENANT GORDON COUNSELMAN."

Alice took it and read:

"Lieutenant Counselman, who died recently at Fort Jefferson, Fla., has left a name among his comrades and in his regiment which any soldier might be proud to own. He was ordered to a Northern post, detailed as professor of Military Science at Colby University. His successor had arrived at Fort Jefferson with his detail, but his command needed him. The dreadful epidemic of yellow-fever was taking off his men. He refused to go; even refused to look at the order for his detail, preferring death at his post to an 'easy berth,' even though that death was facing him in the awful form of pestilence. He chose to remain with his command, and in the words of Colonel Collins, his successor in command, 'stood by while the dead were being carried out, and now lies with ten of the men he tried so hard to save.'

"Subjoined is an order issued by the Gulf Department, an honor rarely paid to a subaltern officer:

"'HEADQUARTERS DEPARTMENT OF THE GULF,
"'HOLLY SPRINGS, MISSISSIPPI.
"'General Orders, No. 27.

"'It is with sincere regret that the Department Commander announces the death at Fort Jefferson, Florida, of First Lieutenant Gordon Counselman of the Third Artillery.

"'This young officer had already won the esteem of his associates and the respect of his commanding officers by his high soldierly qualities, and the circumstances attending his death were such as to furnish a fitting close to his military career.

"'The only officer at an isolated military post when it was visited by a dangerous epidemic, he seemed to multiply himself in his ever-present care and watchfulness for the men of his command, and it is doubtless due to the exhaustion and fatigue resulting from his anxious discharge of duty that he finally fell a victim to the disease.

"'With death on every side and staring him in the face he never faltered in his lonely duty, and when relief finally came he could only welcome it for his men. It came too late to save their faithful commander. Then, and not till then, he yielded to the attack of the destroyer, and on Thursday evening, the 11th of September, died, on duty and at his post.
"'By order of   MAJOR-GENERAL CLARKE.
"''E. R. Carpenter, Ass't. Adjt.-General.'"

Alice handed the paper back to her father.

"It is cruel that you could not know these things first, daughter," he said, kindly.

"No, father. It is just as well. I am glad other

people know them, too. But they will forget. Only *I* shall remember."

But when hosts of letters poured in upon her from Gordon's brother officers and from his countless friends, Alice began to realize, as she never had done before, how he had lived and how he had died. Even she, his own wife, had not known him as these people seemed to have done. For the first time she was getting an outside point of view.

All through the autumn Alice comforted her mother for Gordon's loss. Mrs. Copeland was more bereaved than any one would have suspected. Perhaps she regretted some things. Most people never feel remorse until it is too late.

Gifford hung around Alice with his face grave with sorrow. He filled her room with flowers, and showed her in a thousand ways how his boyish heart ached for her. Everybody said Alice bore up bravely. They never knew how many nights she spent kneeling beside her baby's little bed, her whole soul going up in the anguished cry, " Dear God, why must Thou always take the best?"

Who knows the night-time agony of those who " bear up bravely?"

Alice controlled herself for her mother's sake. Mrs. Copeland could not bear the sight of any grief except her own. Elsie, too, was easily upset.

Kate Vandevoort heard of it in Norway and

came straight home. But it was November before she arrived.

"How will she bear it!" thought Kate. "If I could only see whether she will live by Gordon's life or Mrs. Copeland's."

Kate found Alice a pathetic little black-robed figure sitting beside her mother, both of them engrossed in fancy work. As Kate took Alice in her arms, the ball of worsted rolled under the table and the kitten played with it.

"My poor child," she murmured.

Little Lloyd crept up to Alice, and, pulling at her skirts, said:

"Is my darlin' foddy tummin' home to-day?"

Kate broke into wild weeping.

"Not to-day, dear. Perhaps to-morrow."

THE END

MARK TWAIN'S JOAN OF ARC

PERSONAL RECOLLECTIONS OF JOAN OF ARC. By the Sieur LOUIS DE CONTE (her page and secretary). Freely translated out of the Ancient French into Modern English from the Original Unpublished Manuscript in the National Archives of France, by JEAN FRANÇOIS ALDEN. Illustrated from Original Drawings by F. V. DU MOND, and from Reproductions of Old Paintings and Statues. Crown 8vo, Cloth, Ornamental, $2 50.

One of the most delightful books of the time. It is read with keen enjoyment, and its leaves will be turned over again many times in delicious reminiscence of its fascinating episodes and its entrancing digressions.—RICHARD HENRY STODDARD, in *N. Y. Mail and Express.*

Mark Twain, in the best book he has ever written, has given us a life of Joan of Arc so amazing in its realism, its vividness and force, that, like Shakespeare's plays, it compels acceptance. ... Is not only the best thing he has ever done, but one of the best things done by anybody in fiction for a long time past.—*Speaker*, London.

BY THE SAME AUTHOR:

New Library Editions from New Electrotype Plates. Crown 8vo, Cloth, Ornamental:

THE ADVENTURES OF HUCKLEBERRY FINN. Illustrated. $1 75.

A CONNECTICUT YANKEE IN KING ARTHUR'S COURT. Illustrated. $1 75.

THE PRINCE AND THE PAUPER. Illustrated. $1 75.

LIFE ON THE MISSISSIPPI. Illustrated. $1 75.

TOM SAWYER ABROAD; TOM SAWYER, DETECTIVE; AND OTHER STORIES, ETC. Illustrated. $1 75.

PUBLISHED BY HARPER & BROTHERS, NEW YORK

☞ *For sale by all booksellers, or will be mailed by the publishers, postage prepaid, on receipt of the price.*

By CONSTANCE F. WOOLSON

DOROTHY, and Other Italian Stories. Illustrated. 16mo, Cloth, Ornamental, $1 25.

THE FRONT YARD, and Other Italian Stories. Illustrated. 16mo, Cloth, Ornamental, $1 25.

HORACE CHASE. A Novel. 16mo, Cloth, Ornamental, $1 25.

JUPITER LIGHTS. A Novel. 16mo, Cloth, Ornamental, $1 25.

EAST ANGELS. A Novel. 16mo, Cloth, Ornamental, $1 25.

ANNE. A Novel. Illustrated. 16mo, Cloth, Ornamental, $1 25.

FOR THE MAJOR. A Novelette. 16mo, Cloth, Ornamental, $1 00.

CASTLE NOWHERE. Lake-Country Sketches. 16mo, Cloth, Ornamental, $1 00.

RODMAN THE KEEPER. Southern Sketches. 16mo, Cloth, Ornamental, $1 00.

Characterization is Miss Woolson's forte. Her men and women are not mere puppets, but original, breathing, and finely contrasted creations.—*Chicago Tribune.*

Miss Woolson is one of the few novelists of the day who know how to make conversation, how to individualize the speakers, how to exclude rabid realism without falling into literary formality.—*N. Y. Tribune.*

'For tenderness and purity of thought, for exquisitely delicate sketching of characters, Miss Woolson is unexcelled among writers of fiction.—*New Orleans Picayune.*

MENTONE, CAIRO, AND CORFU. Illustrated. Post 8vo, Cloth, Ornamental, $1 75.

For swiftly graphic stroke, for delicacy of appreciative coloring, and for sentimental suggestiveness, it would be hard to rival Miss Woolson's sketches.—*Watchman,* Boston.

To the accuracy of a guide-book it adds the charm of a cultured and appreciative vision.—*Philadelphia Ledger.*

PUBLISHED BY HARPER & BROTHERS, NEW YORK

☞ *The above works are for sale by all booksellers, or will be sent by the publishers, postage prepaid, on receipt of the price.*

By RICHARD HARDING DAVIS

THREE GRINGOS IN VENEZUELA AND CENTRAL AMERICA. Illustrated. Post 8vo, Cloth, $1 50.

Mr. Davis is an indefatigable traveller and a delightful raconteur. . . . His books upon European travel are as good as any of modern times, and this new volume about a country which is now prominent is very interesting.—*Observer, N. Y.*

ABOUT PARIS. Illustrated. Post 8vo, Cloth, $1 25.

A book of sketches, graceful and interesting, recommended by the freshness and vivacity of their view and manner.—*N. Y. Sun.*

THE PRINCESS ALINE. Illustrated. Post 8vo, Cloth, $1 25.

The style is charming, and there is a delicate and romantic treatment which runs throughout the narrative.—*Churchman, N. Y.*

THE EXILES, AND OTHER STORIES. Illustrated. Post 8vo, Cloth, $1 50.

These varying but uniformly characteristic tales show the travelled man, they show the observing man, and they show the natural and well-trained story-teller.—*Interior,* Chicago.

OUR ENGLISH COUSINS. Ill'd. Post 8vo, Cloth, $1 25.

Admirable examples of genuine observation recorded with the light and quick, yet firm, clear touch of a literary artist.—*Philadelphia Times.*

THE RULERS OF THE MEDITERRANEAN. Illustrated. Post 8vo, Cloth, $1 25.

Mr. Davis has combined history, geography, and romance in such a way as to leave no dull or stupid line or passage in his book.—*San Francisco Chronicle.*

THE WEST FROM A CAR-WINDOW. Illustrated. Post 8vo, Cloth, $1 25.

The United States soldier commissioned and enlisted, and the American Indian alike, have cause to be grateful for the fate that drew them into the line of vision of such a delineator.—*Nation, N. Y.*

VAN BIBBER, AND OTHERS. Illustrated. Post 8vo, Cloth, $1 00; Paper, 60 cents.

Short stories so full of life and significance that they often seem to tell us more of the social conditions they describe, within ten or twelve pages, than our own novelists can compress into a volume.—*Spectator,* London.

PUBLISHED BY HARPER & BROTHERS, NEW YORK

☞ *For sale by all booksellers, or will be mailed by the publishers, postage prepaid, on receipt of the price.*

HARPER'S AMERICAN ESSAYISTS

OTHER TIMES AND OTHER SEASONS. By LAURENCE HUTTON.
A LITTLE ENGLISH GALLERY. By LOUISE IMOGEN GUINEY.
LITERARY AND SOCIAL SILHOUETTES. By HJALMAR HJORTH BOYESEN.
STUDIES OF THE STAGE. By BRANDER MATTHEWS.
AMERICANISMS AND BRITICISMS, with Other Essays on Other Isms. By BRANDER MATTHEWS.
AS WE GO. By CHARLES DUDLEY WARNER. With Illustrations.
AS WE WERE SAYING. By CHARLES DUDLEY WARNER. With Illustrations.
FROM THE EASY CHAIR. By GEORGE WILLIAM CURTIS.
FROM THE EASY CHAIR. *Second Series.* By GEORGE WILLIAM CURTIS.
FROM THE EASY CHAIR. *Third Series.* By GEORGE WILLIAM CURTIS.
CRITICISM AND FICTION. By WILLIAM DEAN HOWELLS.
FROM THE BOOKS OF LAURENCE HUTTON.
CONCERNING ALL OF US. By THOMAS WENTWORTH HIGGINSON.
THE WORK OF JOHN RUSKIN. By CHARLES WALDSTEIN.
PICTURE AND TEXT. By HENRY JAMES. With Illustrations.

16mo, Cloth, $1 00 each. Complete Sets, in White and Gold, $1 25 a Volume.

PUBLISHED BY HARPER & BROTHERS, NEW YORK.

☞ *The above works are for sale by all booksellers, or will be mailed by the publishers, postage prepaid, on receipt of the price.*

THE ODD NUMBER SERIES

16mo, Cloth, Ornamental

BLACK DIAMONDS. By Maurus Jokai. Translated by Frances A. Gerard. With Portrait. $1 50.

DOÑA PERFECTA. By B. Pérez Galdós. Translated by Mary J. Serrano. With Portrait. $1 00.

PARISIAN POINTS OF VIEW. Nine Tales by Ludovic Halévy. Translated by Edith V. B. Matthews. With Portrait. $1 00.

DAME CARE. By Hermann Sudermann. Translated by Bertha Overbeck. With Portrait. $1 00.

TALES OF TWO COUNTRIES. By Alexander Kielland. Translated by William Archer. With Portrait. $1 00.

TEN TALES BY FRANÇOIS COPPÉE. Translated by Walter Learned. With Portrait and 50 Illustrations by A. E. Sterner. $1 25.

MODERN GHOSTS. Selected and Translated from the Works of Guy de Maupassant, Pedro Antonio de Alarçon, Alexander Kielland, and Others. $1 00.

THE HOUSE BY THE MEDLAR-TREE. By Giovanni Verga. Translated from the Italian by Mary A. Craig. $1 00.

PASTELS IN PROSE. Translated by Stuart Merrill. 150 Illustrations by H. W. McVickar. $1 25.

MARÍA: A South American Romance. By Jorge Isaacs. Translated by Rollo Ogden. $1 00.

THE ODD NUMBER. Thirteen Tales by Guy de Maupassant. The Translation by Jonathan Sturges. With Portrait. $1 00.

Pastels in Prose, Coppée's Tales, and The Odd Number—Three Volumes—White and Gold, in a Box, $5 25 per set.

Published by HARPER & BROTHERS, New York.

☞ *The above works are for sale by all booksellers, or will be mailed by the publishers, postage prepaid, on receipt of the price.*

By JOHN KENDRICK BANGS

THE BICYCLERS, AND THREE OTHER FARCES. Illustrated. 16mo, Cloth, Ornamental, $1 25.

> The farces are crowded with comic situations, brilliant repartee, and wholesome fun.—*Brooklyn Standard-Union.*

A HOUSE-BOAT ON THE STYX. Being Some Account of the Divers Doings of the Associated Shades. Illustrated. 16mo, Cloth, Ornamental, $1 25.

> Well worth reading. . . . It is full of genuine crisp humor. It is the best work of length Mr. Bangs has yet done, and he is to be congratulated.—*N. Y. Mail and Express.*

MR. BONAPARTE OF CORSICA. Illustrated by H. W. McVICKAR. 16mo, Cloth, Ornamental, $1 25.

> Mr. Bangs is probably the generator of more hearty, healthful, purely good-humored laughs than any other half-dozen men of our country to-day.—*Interior, Chicago.*

THE IDIOT. Illustrated. 16mo, Cloth, Ornamental, $1 00.

> "The Idiot" continues to be as amusing and as triumphantly bright in the volume called after his name as in "Coffee and Repartee."—*Evangelist, N. Y.*

THE WATER GHOST, AND OTHERS. Illustrated. 16mo, Cloth, Ornamental, $1 25.

> The funny side of the ghost genre is brought out with originality, and, considering the morbidity that surrounds the subject, it is a wholesome thing to offer the public a series of tales letting in the sunlight of laughter.—*Hartford Courant.*

THREE WEEKS IN POLITICS. Illustrated. 32mo, Cloth, Ornamental, 50 cents.

> He who can read this narrative of a campaigners' trials without laughing must be a stoic indeed.—*Philadelphia Bulletin.*

COFFEE AND REPARTEE. Illustrated. 32mo, Cloth, Ornamental, 50 cents.

> Is delightfully free from conventionality; is breezy, witty, and possessed of an originality both genial and refreshing.—*Saturday Evening Gazette, Boston.*

PUBLISHED BY HARPER & BROTHERS, NEW YORK

☞ *For sale by all booksellers, or will be mailed by the publishers, postage prepaid, on receipt of the price.*

DATE DUE

GAYLORD			PRINTED IN U S A

www.ingramcontent.com/pod-product-compliance
Lightning Source LLC
Chambersburg PA
CBHW021351230426
43666CB00006B/479